POP FAVORITES for Fingerstyle Guitar

Contents

ISBN 978-1-60378-434-4

Copyright © 2013 Cherry Lane Music Company
International Copyright Secured   All Rights Reserved

Visit our website at www.cherrylaneprint.com

Afternoon Delight

Words and Music by Bill Danoff

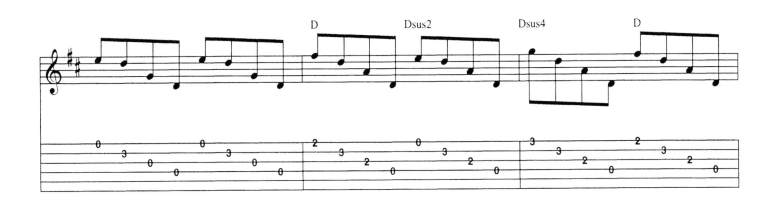

Gon - na find my ba - by, gon - na

hold her tight, gon - na grab some af - ter - noon⎯ de - light.⎯ My

mot - to's al - ways been, "When it's right, it's right." Why wait un - til the mid - dle of a

cold, dark night, when ev - 'ry - thing's a lit - tle clear - er in the

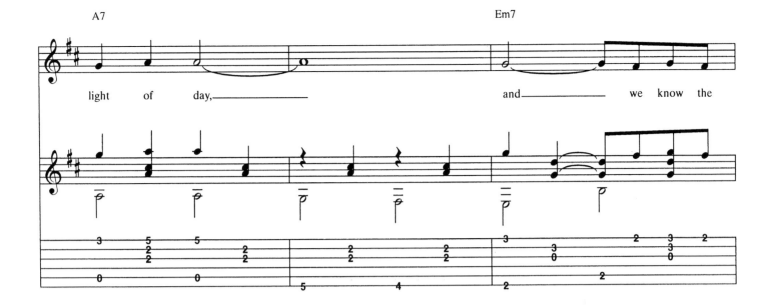

light of day,_____ and_____ we know the

night is al - ways gon - na be here an - y - way?_____

Think - ing of you's work - ing up my ap - pe - tite, look - ing for - ward to a lit - tle af - ter -
out this morn - ing feel - ing so po - lite, I al - ways thought a fish could not be caught who

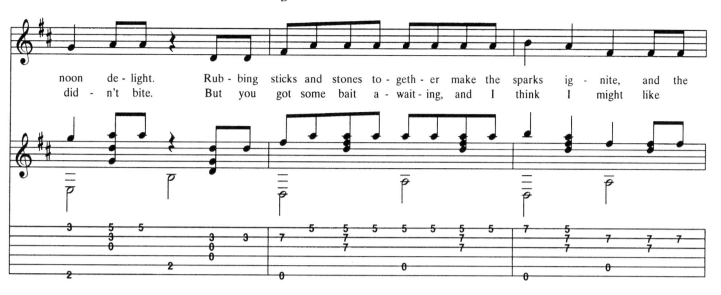

noon de - light. Rub - bing sticks and stones to - geth - er make the sparks ig - nite, and the
did - n't bite. But you got some bait a - wait - ing, and I think I might like

thought of rub - bing you is get - ting so ex - cit - ing.
nib - bl - ing a lit - tle af - ter - noon de - light.⎫ Sky - rock - ets in
⎭

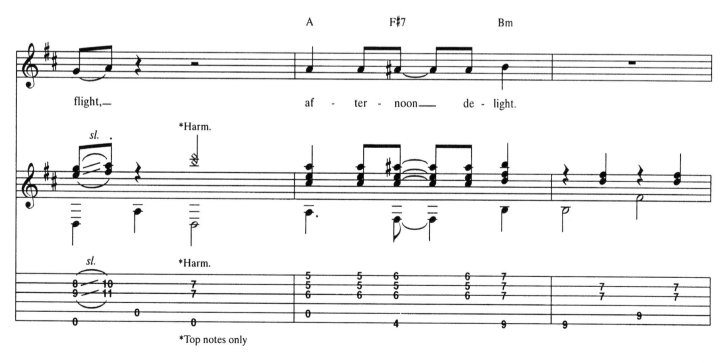

flight,— af - ter - noon— de - light.

*Harm.

sl.

*Harm.

*Top notes only

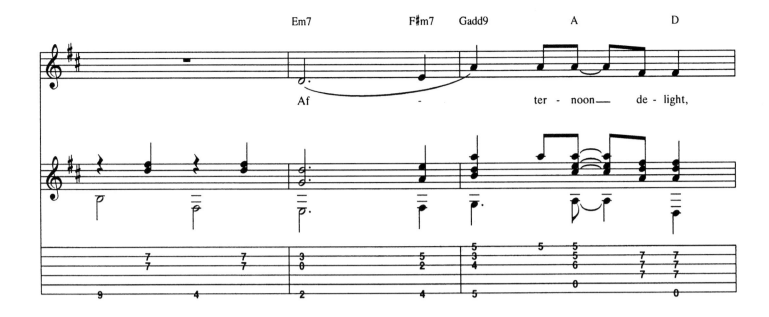

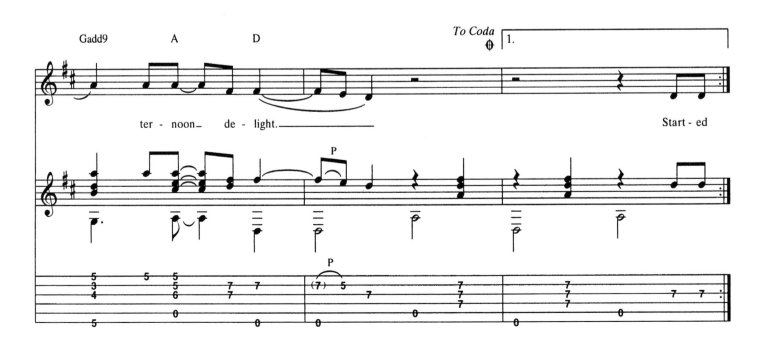

Be waiting for me, ba - by, when I

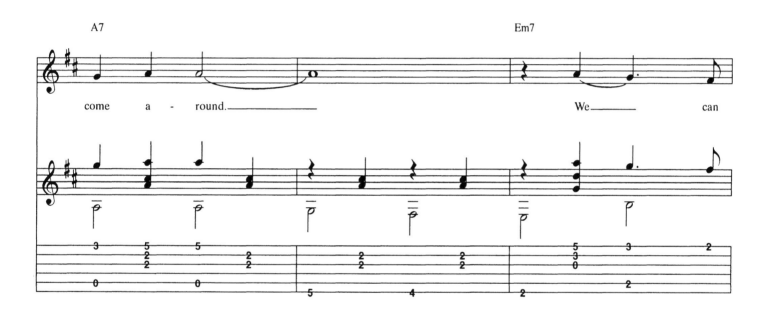

come a - round. We can

D.S. (lyric 1) al Coda

make a lot of lov - ing 'fore the sun gone down.

Coda

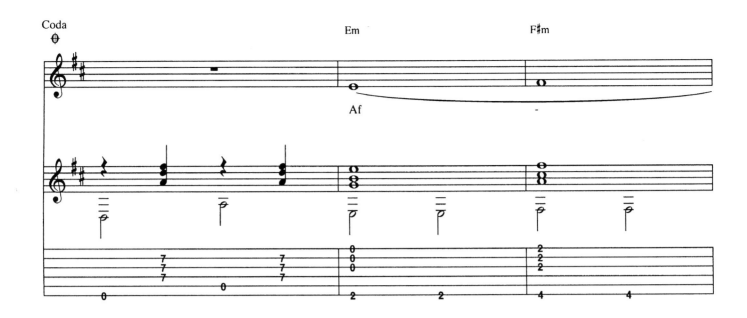

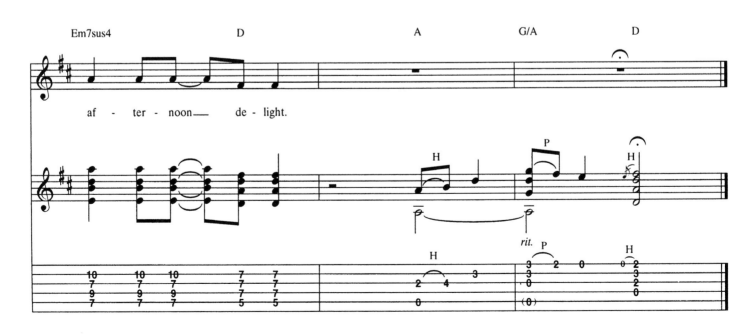

Daydream Believer

featured in the Television Series THE MONKEES

Words and Music by John Stewart

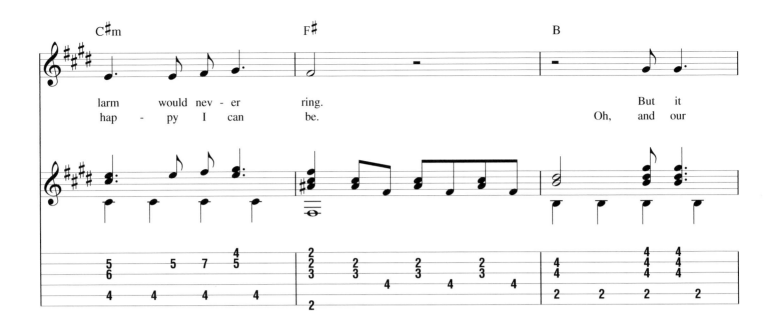

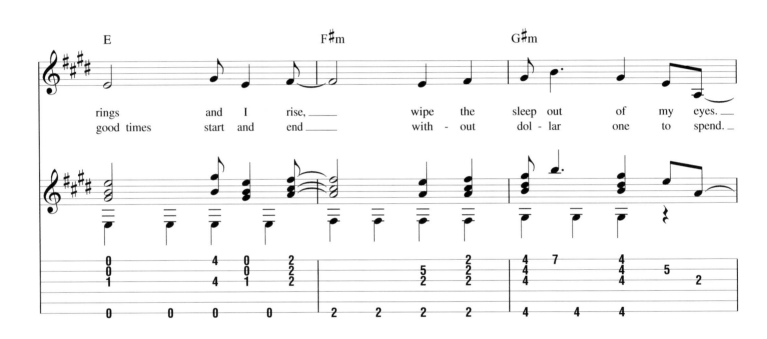

10

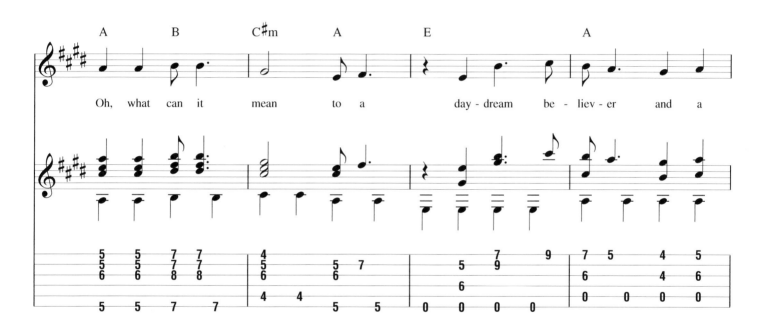

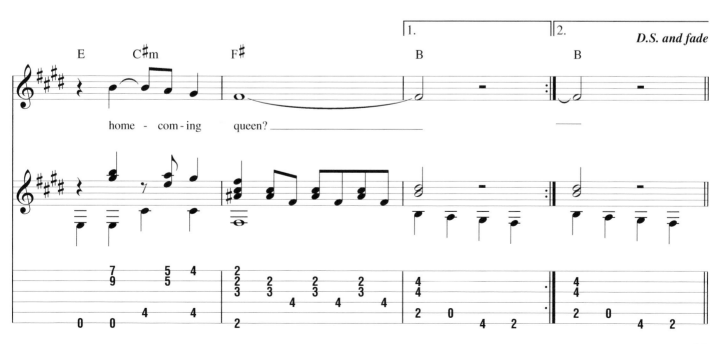

Eleanor Rigby

Words and Music by John Lennon and Paul McCartney

Drop D tuning:
(low to high) D-A-D-G-B-E

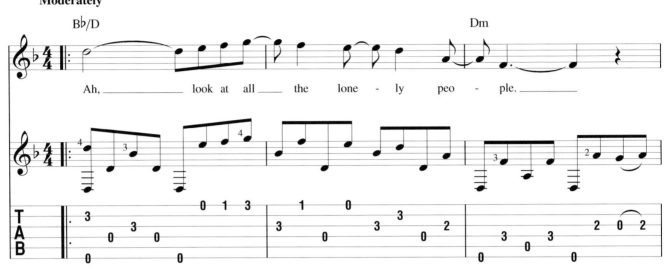

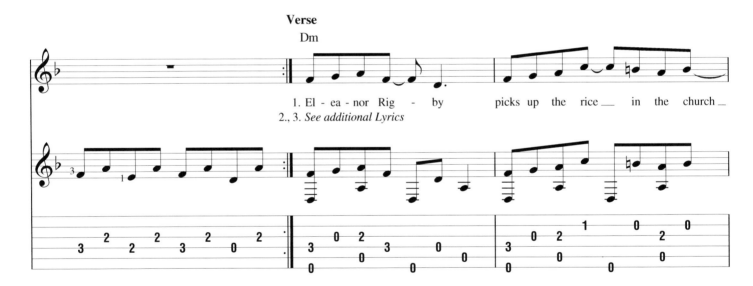

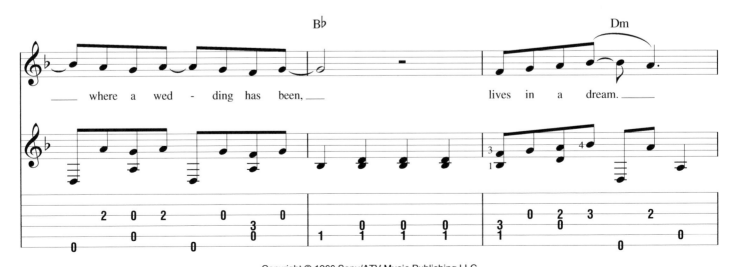

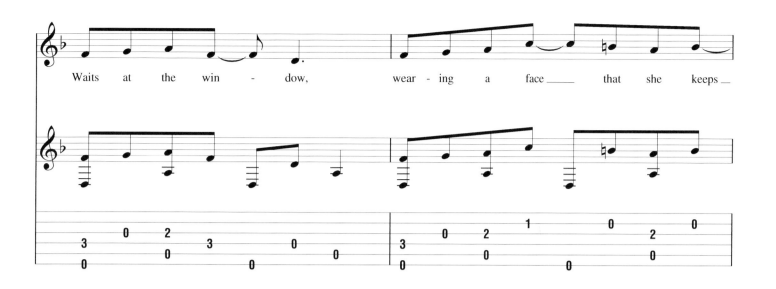

Chorus

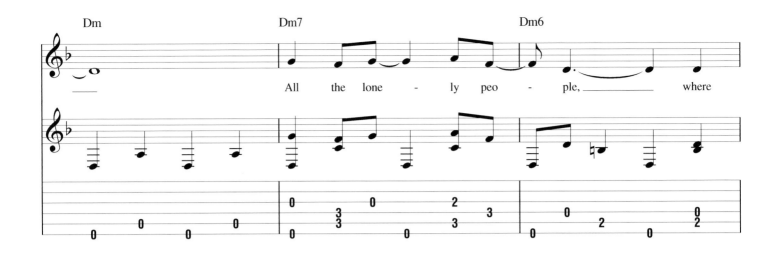

All the lone - ly peo - ple, _____ where

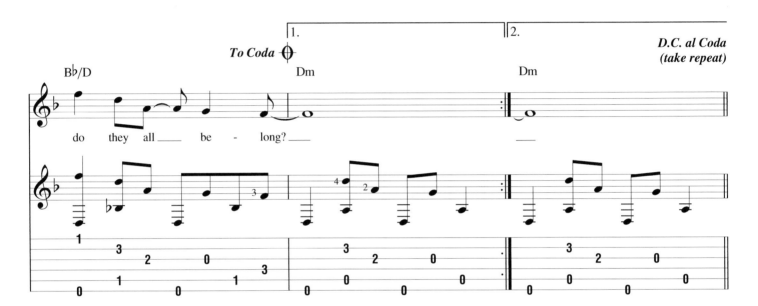

To Coda ⊕   D.C. al Coda (take repeat)

do they all ___ be - long? ___

⊕ Coda

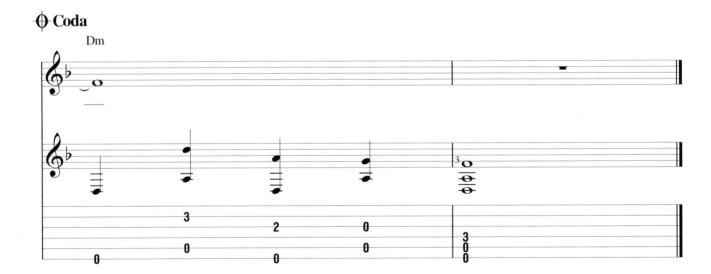

Additional Lyrics

2. Father McKenzie, writing the words of a sermon that no one will hear,
   No one comes near.
   Look at him working, darning his socks in the night when there's nobody there.
   What does he care?

3. Eleanor Rigby died in the church and was buried along with her name,
   Nobody came.
   Father McKenzie, wiping the dirt from his hands as he walks from the grave,
   No one was saved.

From a Distance

Words and Music by Julie Gold

flight.
feed.
for.

From — a dis - tance there___ is har -
From — a dis - tance we___ are in -
From — a dis - tance there___ is har -

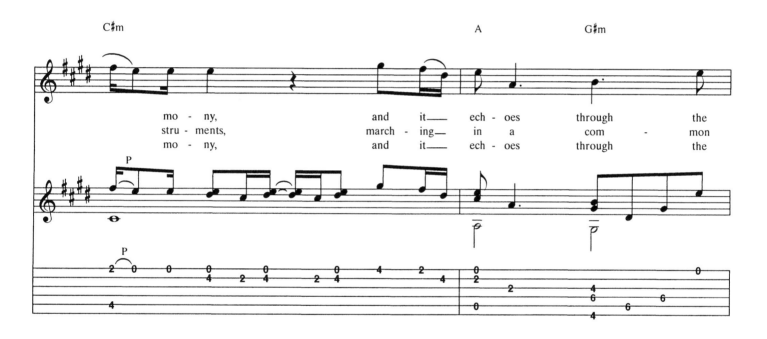

mo - ny, and it__ ech - oes through the
stru - ments, march - ing__ in a com - mon
mo - ny, and it__ ech - oes through the

land.___ It's the voice of__ hope,___ it's the
band.___ Play - ing songs of__ hope,___ play - ing
land.___ It's the hope of__ hopes,___ it's the

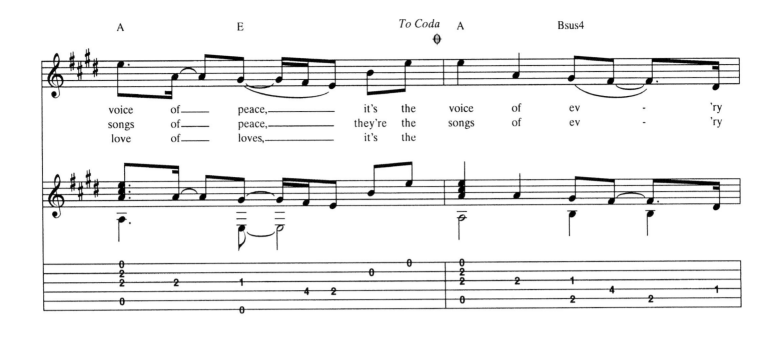

voice of___ peace,_____ it's the voice of ev - 'ry
songs of___ peace,_____ they're the songs of ev - 'ry
love of___ loves,_____ it's the

man.   From a

man.   God_ is watch - ing us,___ God_ is

watch - ing us, God— is watch - ing us from a dis - tance.—

19

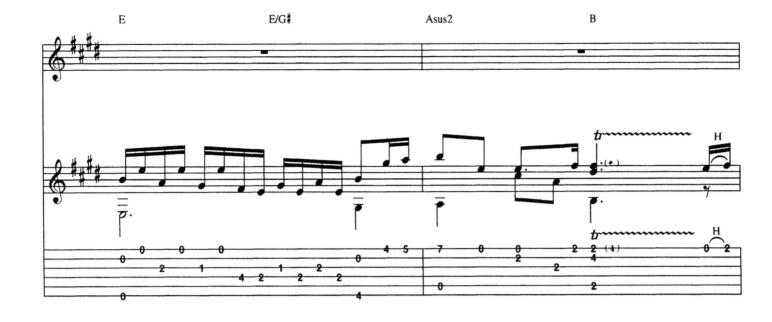

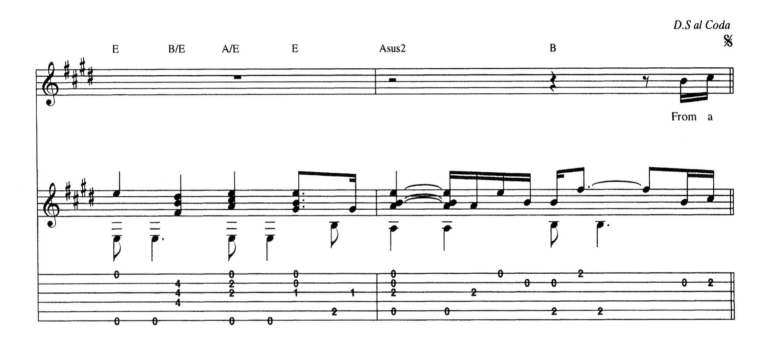

From a

heart_____ of ev - 'ry__ man. It's the

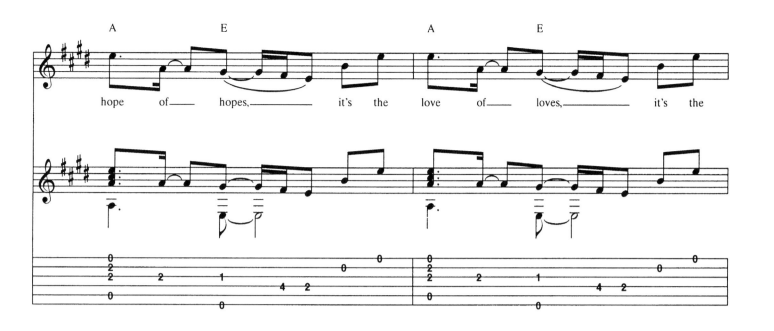

hope of ___ hopes, _____ it's the love of ___ loves, _____ it's the

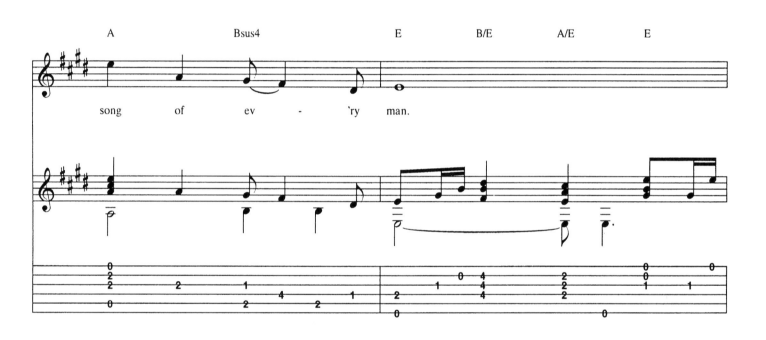

song of ev - 'ry man.

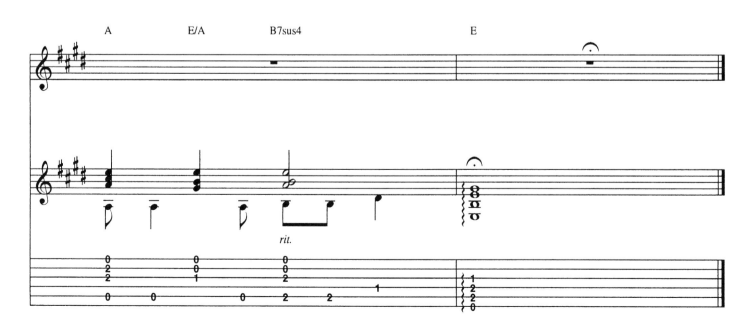

rit.

The Heart of Life

Words and Music by John Mayer

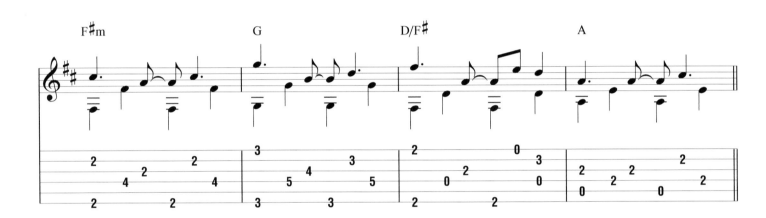

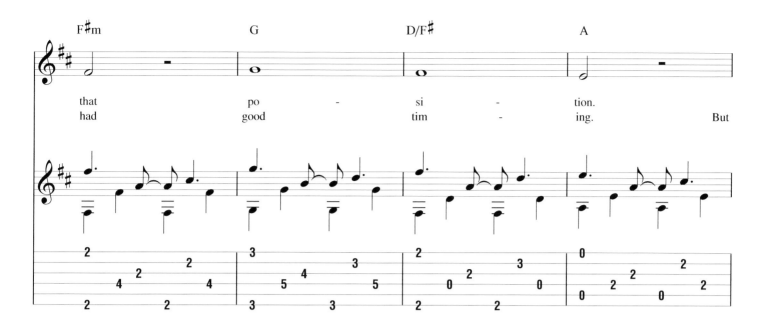

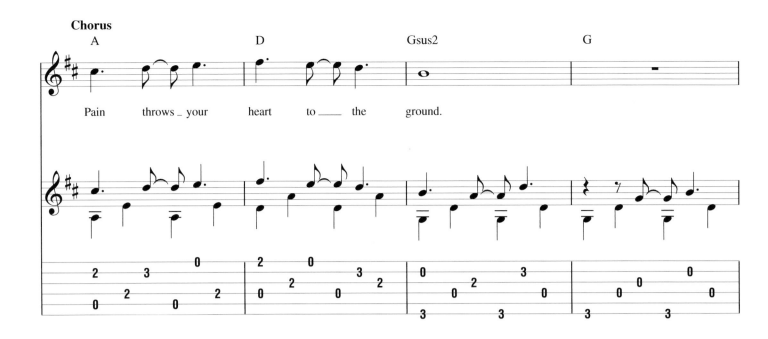

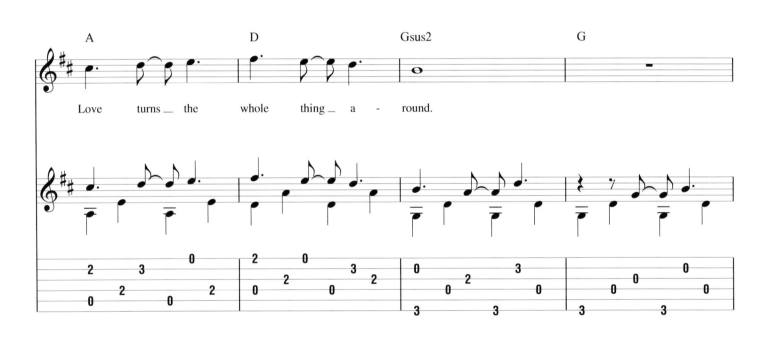

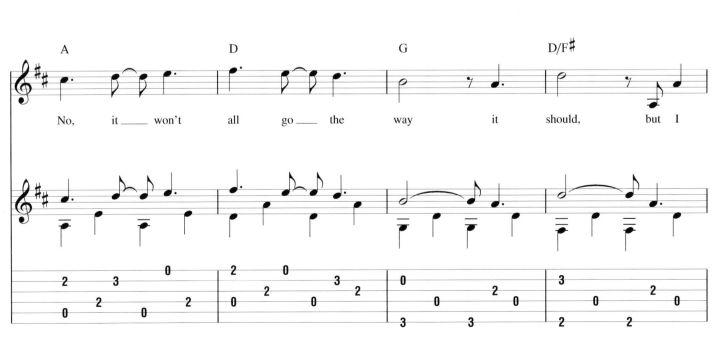

know _____ the heart of life _____ is good.

Coda
Chorus

Pain throws _ your heart _____ to the ground. _____

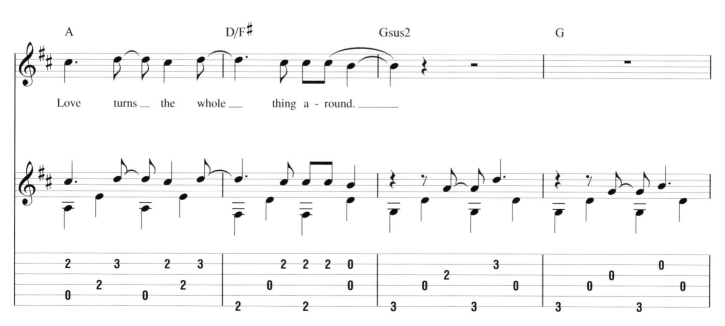

Love turns _ the whole _____ thing a - round. _____

Fear is ___ a friend who's ___ mis - un - der - stood, but I

know ___ the heart of life ___ is good. I know it's good. ___

Repeat and fade

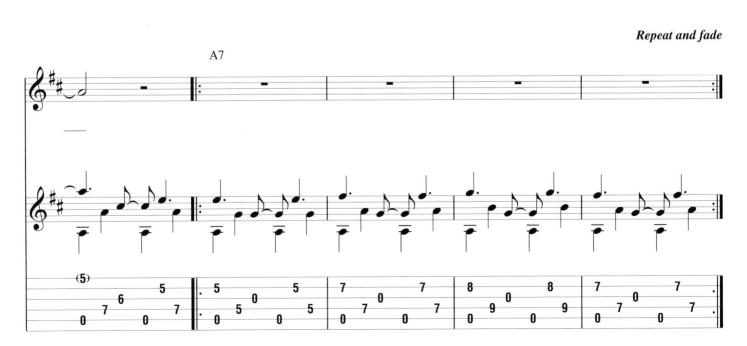

How Deep Is Your Love

from the Motion Picture SATURDAY NIGHT FEVER
Words and Music by Barry Gibb, Robin Gibb and Maurice Gibb

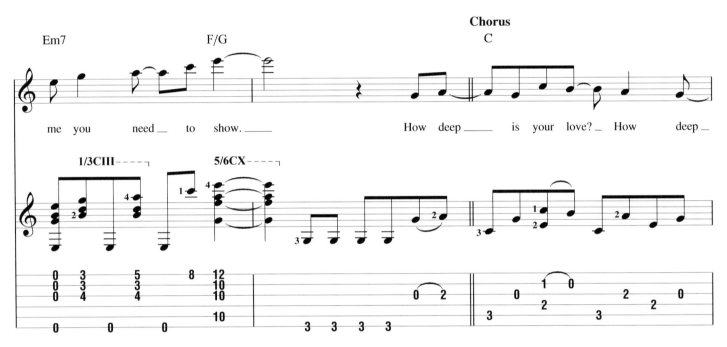

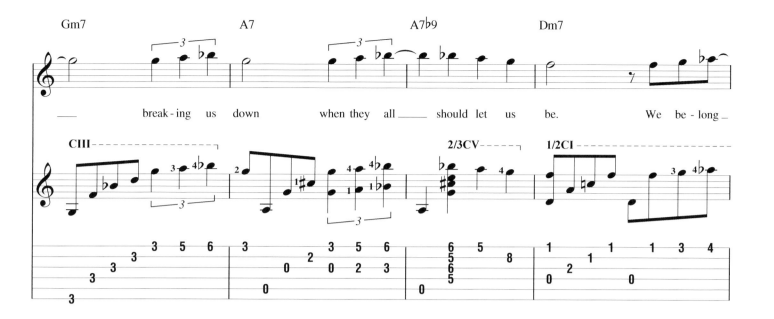

break-ing us down   when they all ___ should let us   be.   We be - long ___

Outro

___ to you ___ and   me.

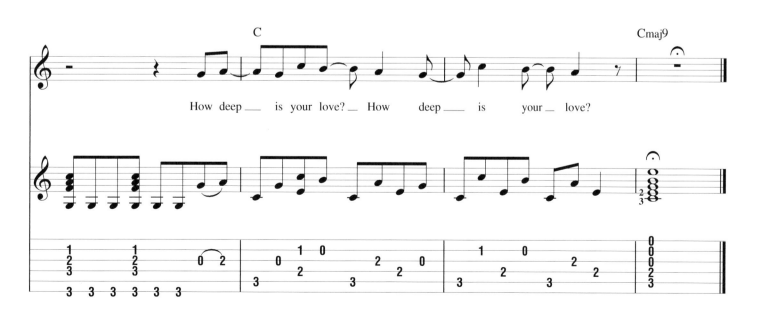

How deep ___ is your love? ___ How   deep ___ is   your ___ love?

Human Nature

Words and Music by John Bettis and Steve Porcaro

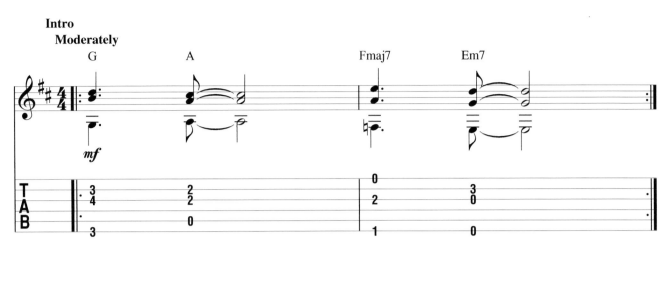

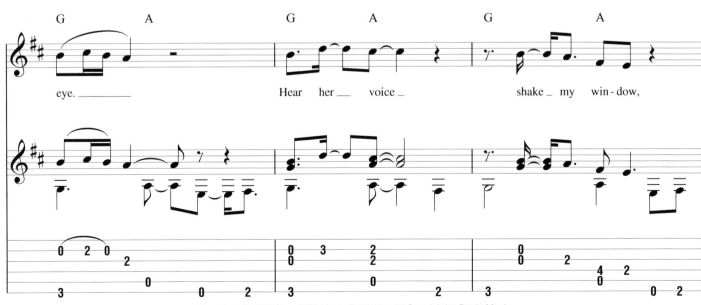

sweet __ se - duc - ing _____ sighs.

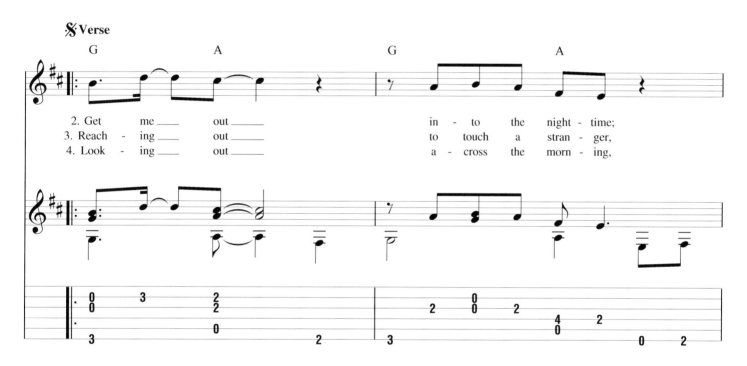

% **Verse**

2. Get me __ out _____ in - to the night - time;
3. Reach - ing __ out _____ to touch a stran - ger,
4. Look - ing __ out _____ a - cross the morn - ing,

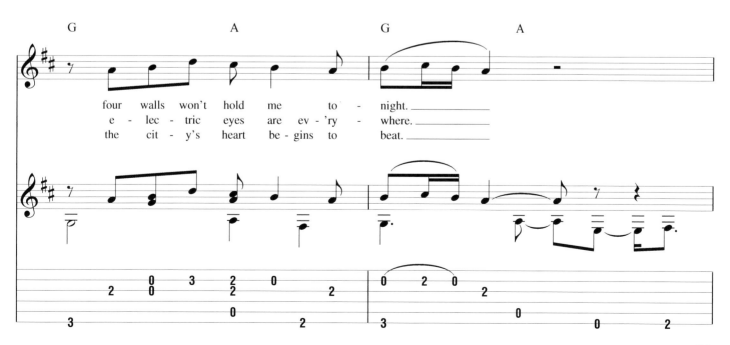

four walls won't hold me to - night. _____
e - lec - tric eyes are ev - 'ry - where. _____
the cit - y's heart be - gins to beat. _____

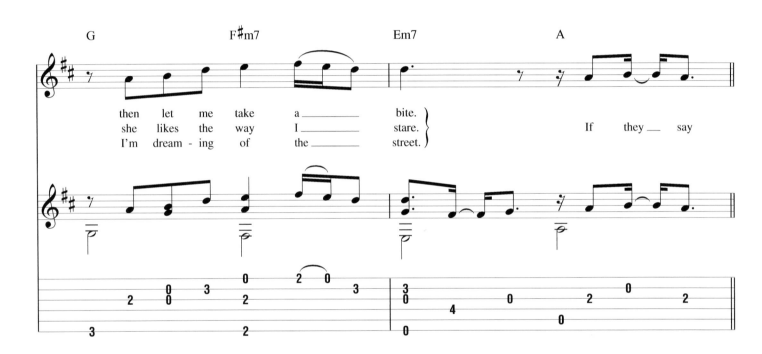

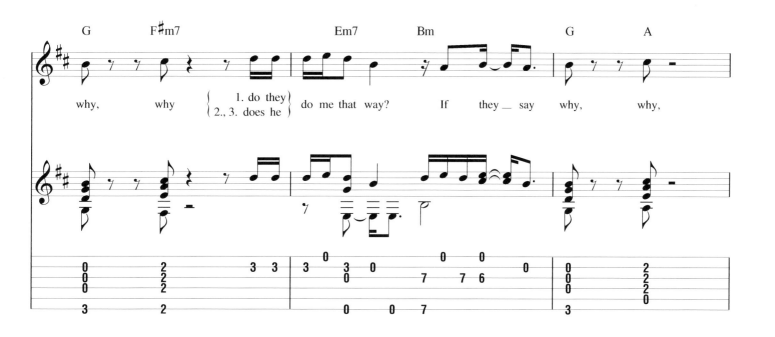

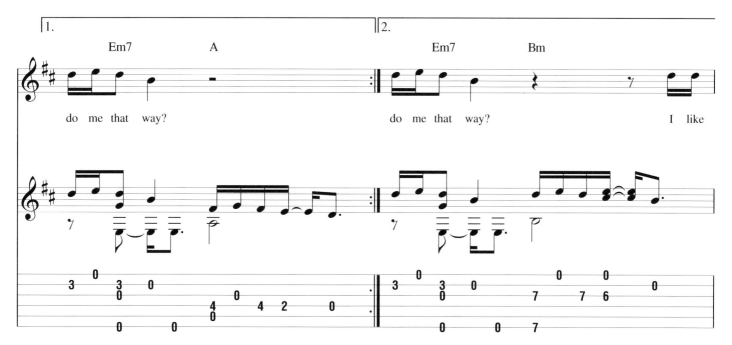

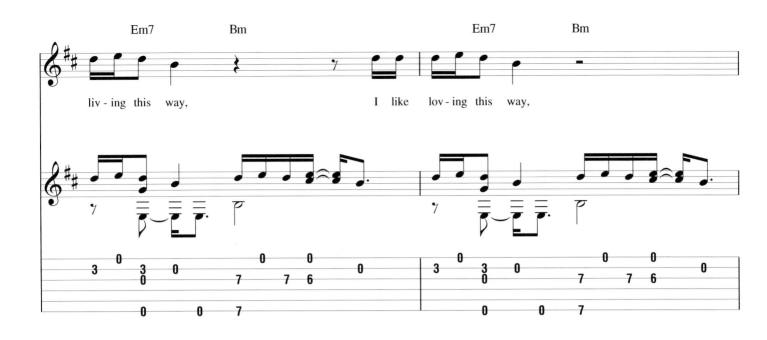

liv - ing this way,   I like lov - ing this way,

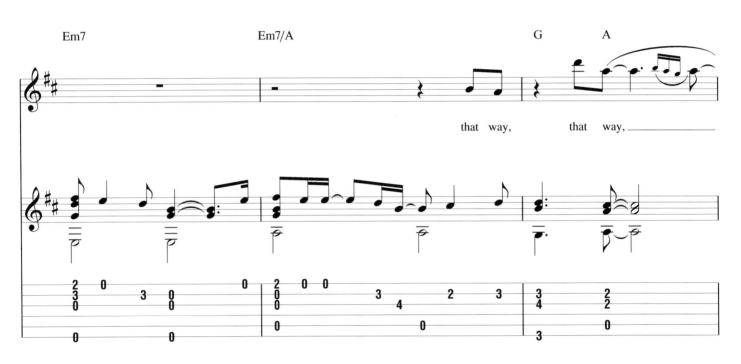

that way,   that way, _____

D.S. al Coda

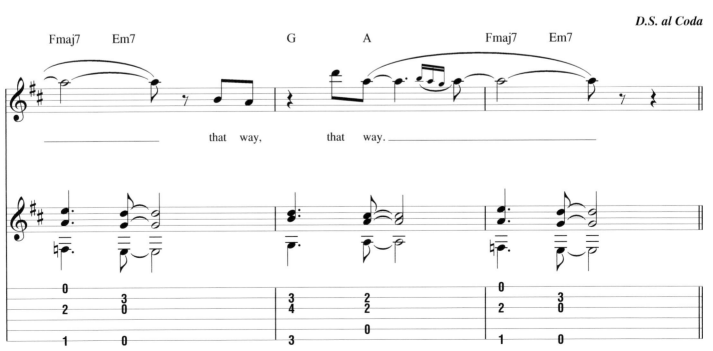

that way,   that way. _____

⊕ Coda

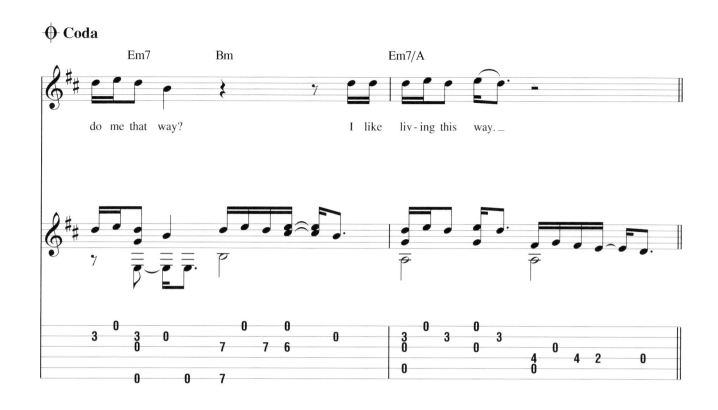

do me that way? I like liv-ing this way. _

Outro

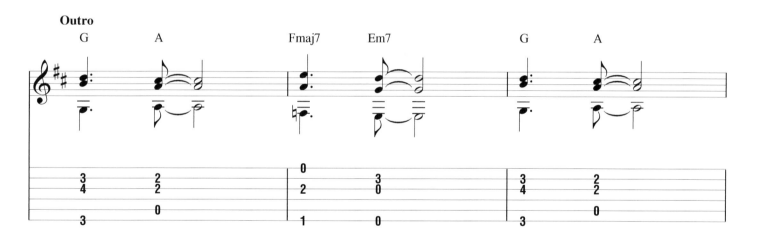

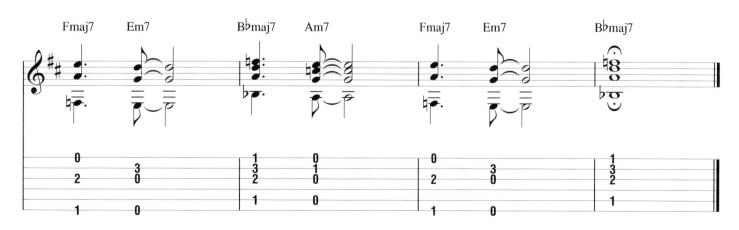

Just the Way You Are

featured in MOVIN' OUT

Words and Music by Billy Joel

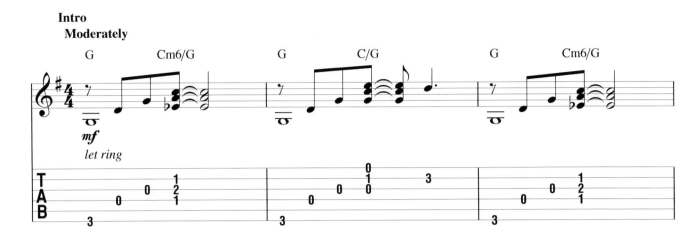

1. Don't go chang - ing
3. Don't go try - ing
7. *Instrumental…*

to try and please ___ me;
some new fash - ion;

you nev - er
don't change the

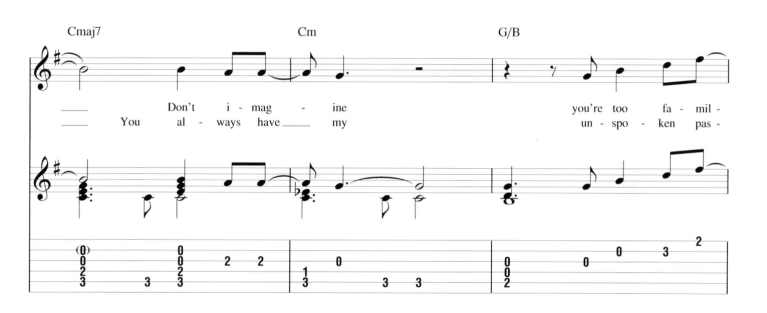

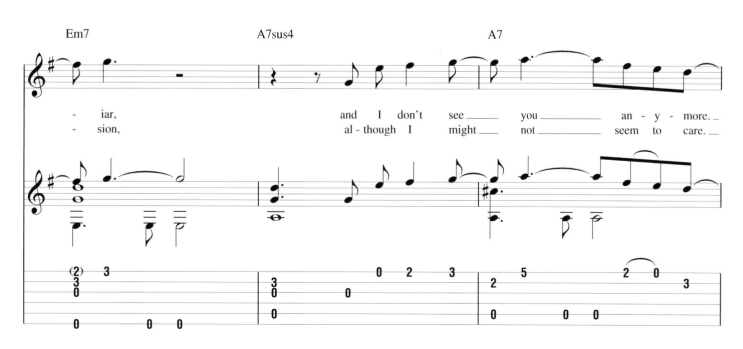

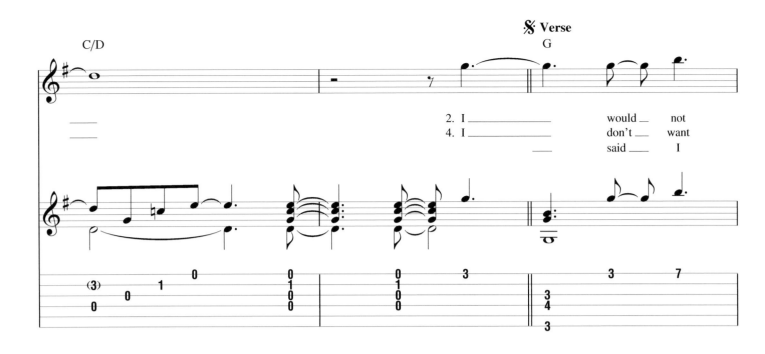

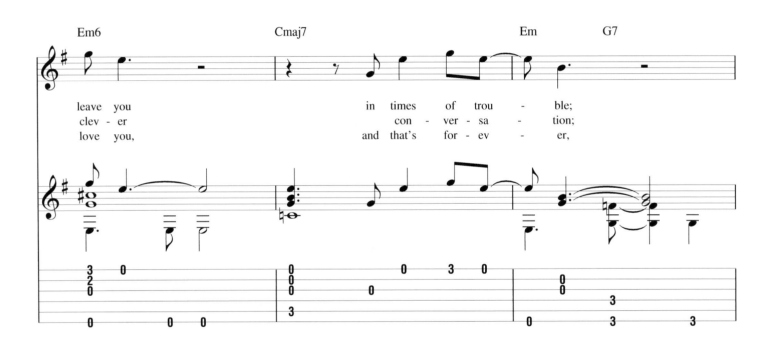

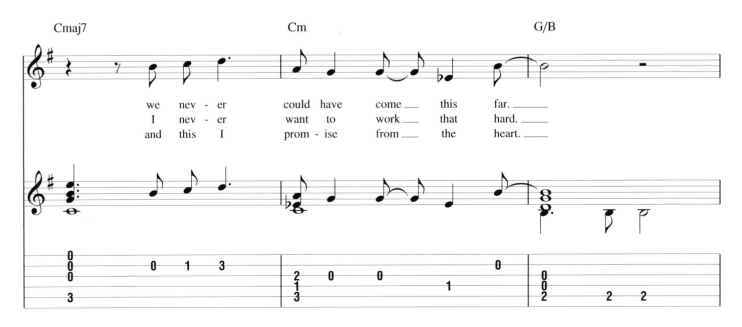

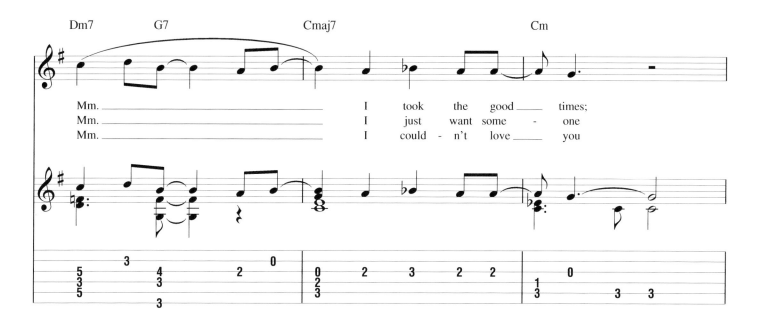

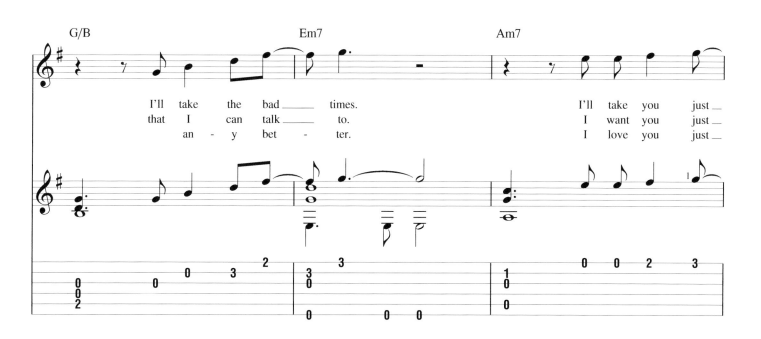

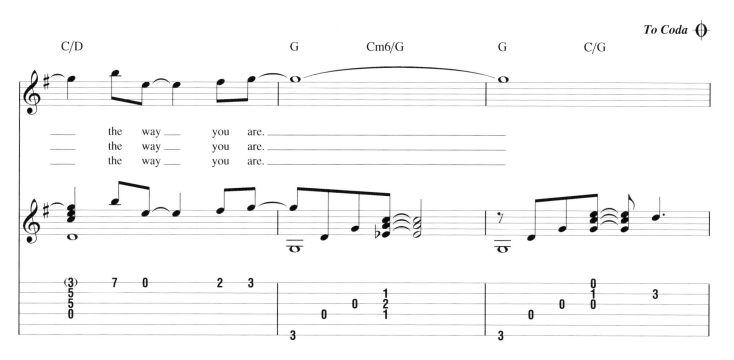

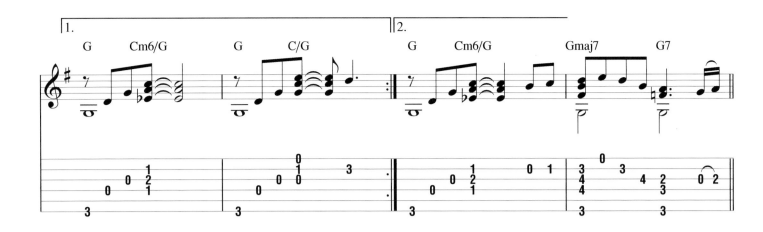

Bridge

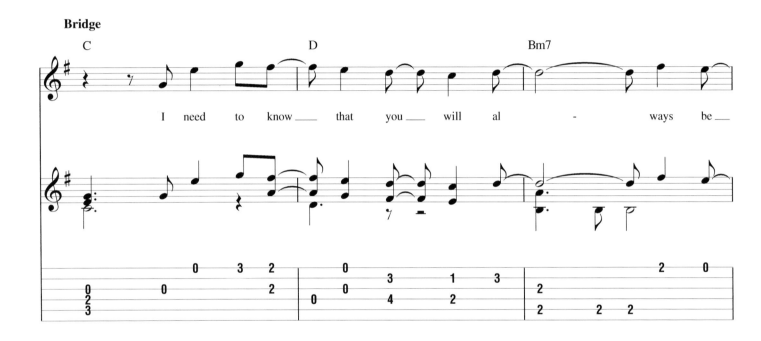

I need to know ____ that you ____ will al - ways be ____

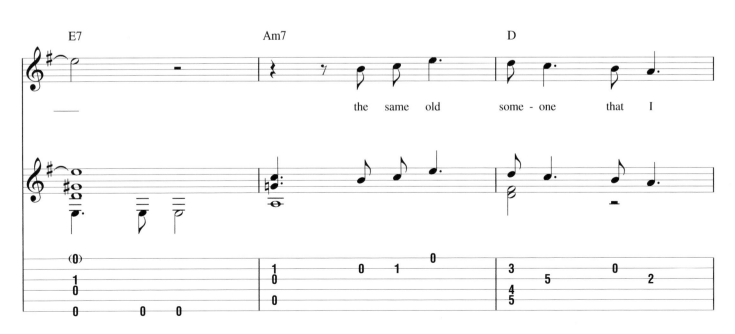

the same old some - one that I

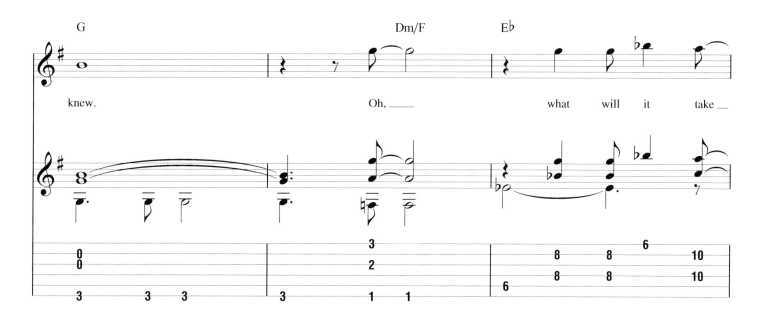

knew. Oh, _____ what will it take _____

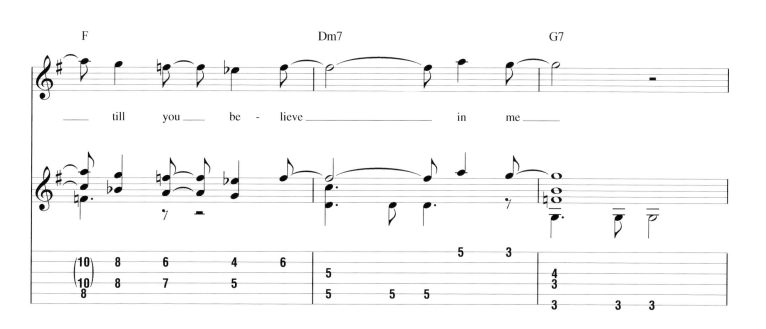

_____ till you _____ be - lieve _____ in me _____

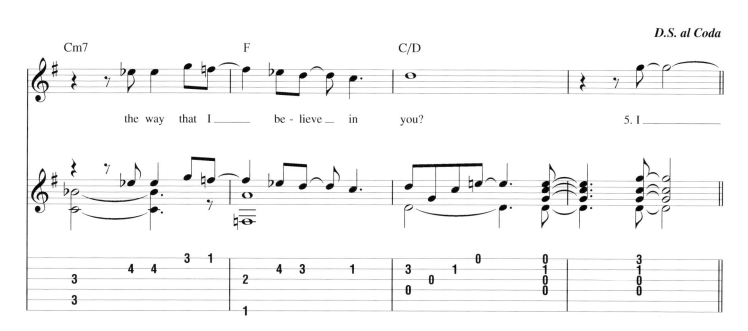

the way that I _____ be - lieve _____ in you?

D.S. al Coda

5. I _____

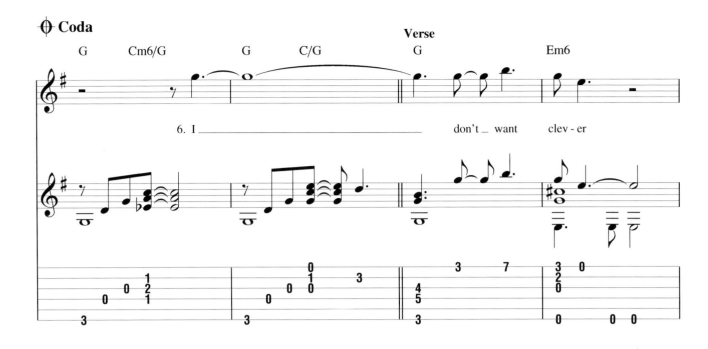

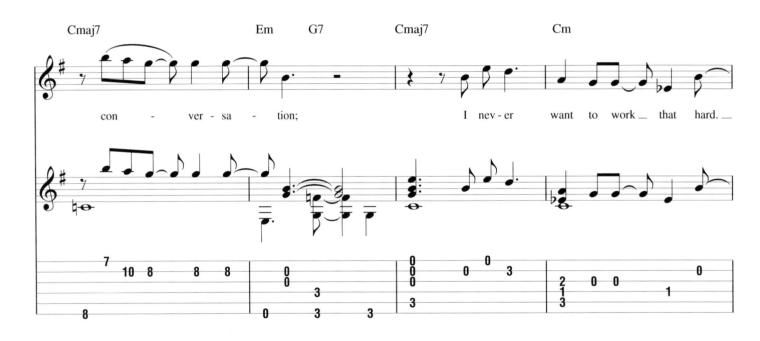

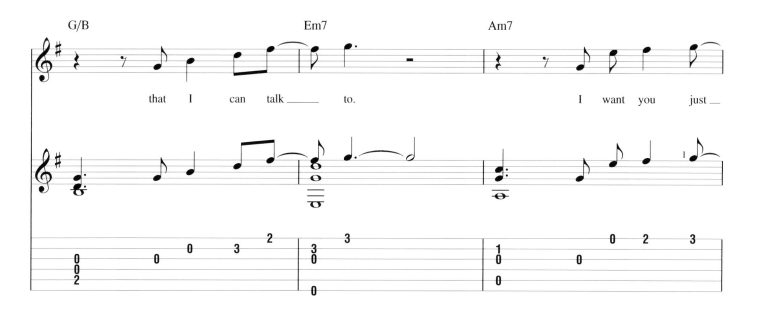

that I can talk____ to.   I want you just____

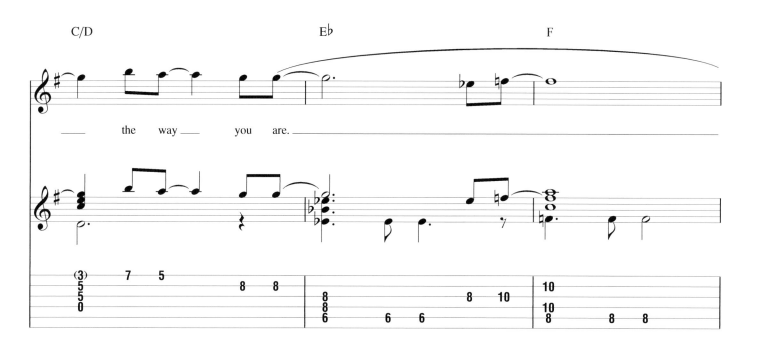

____ the way____ you are._____

D.S.S. (instrumental) and fade

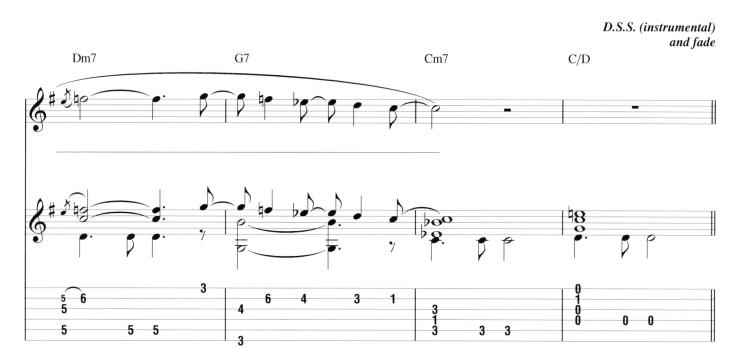

Kodachrome™

Words and Music by Paul Simon

Intro
Moderately fast

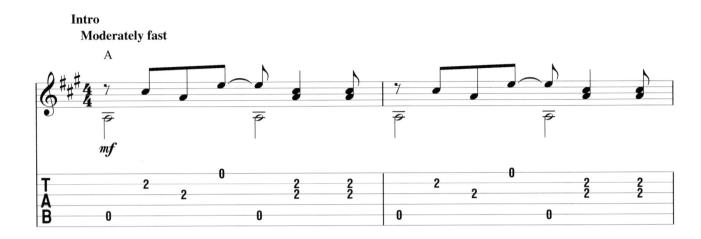

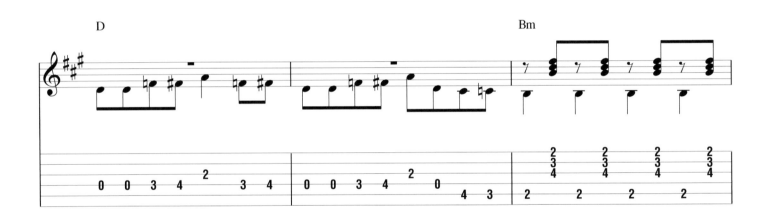

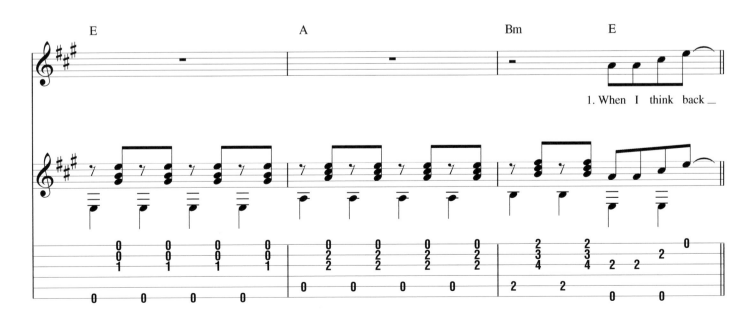

1. When I think back ___

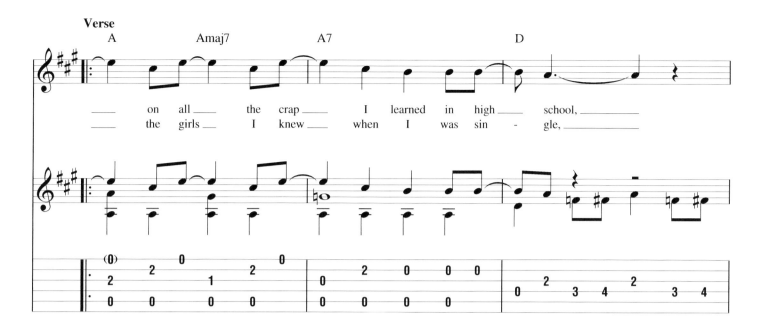

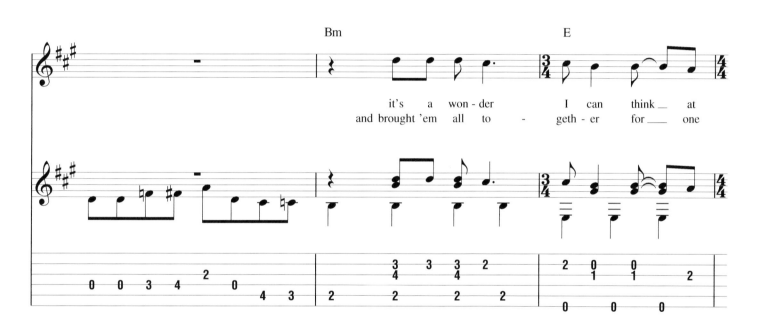

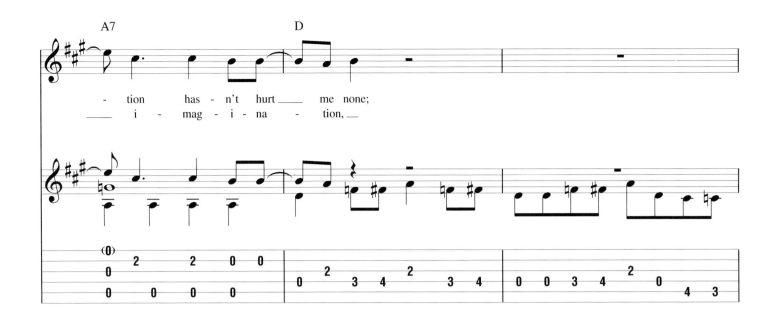

-tion has -n't hurt ___ me none;
___ i - mag - i - na - tion, ___

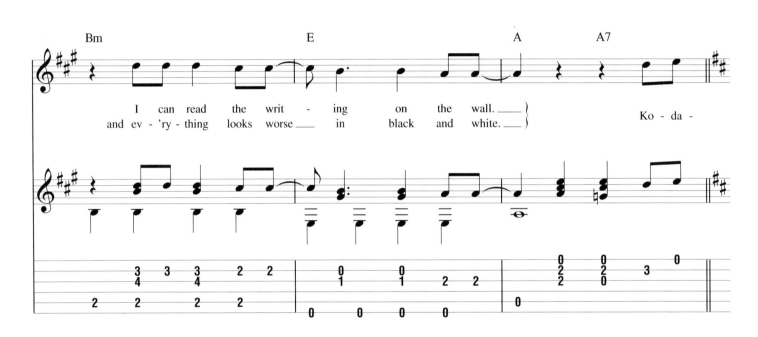

I can read the writ - ing on the wall. ___
and ev - 'ry - thing looks worse ___ in black and white. ___

Ko - da -

Chorus

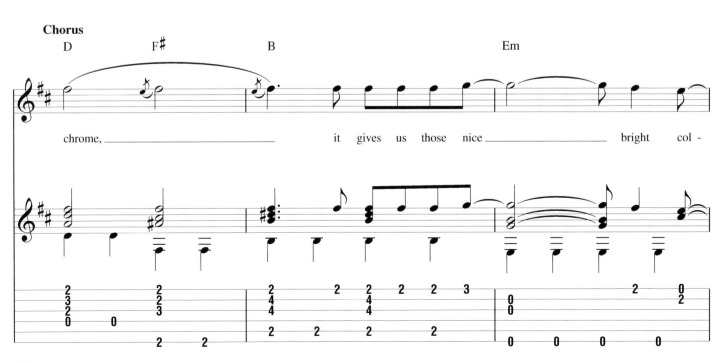

chrome, _____ it gives us those nice _____ bright col -

46

-ors; it gives us the greens _____ of sum - mers, makes you think all _____ the

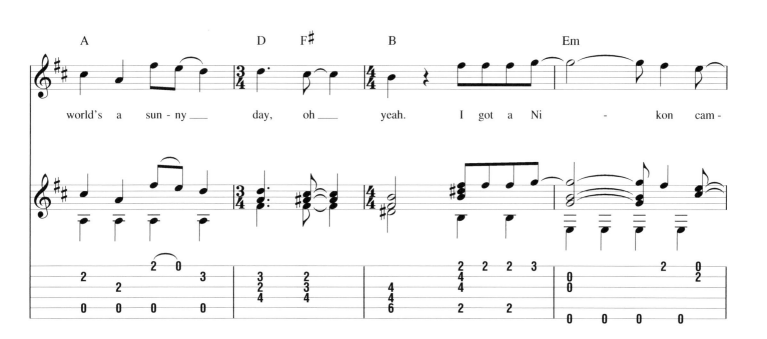

world's a sun - ny _____ day, oh _____ yeah. I got a Ni - kon cam-

-'ra; I love to take a pho - to - graph, _____ so, ma - ma, don't take _____

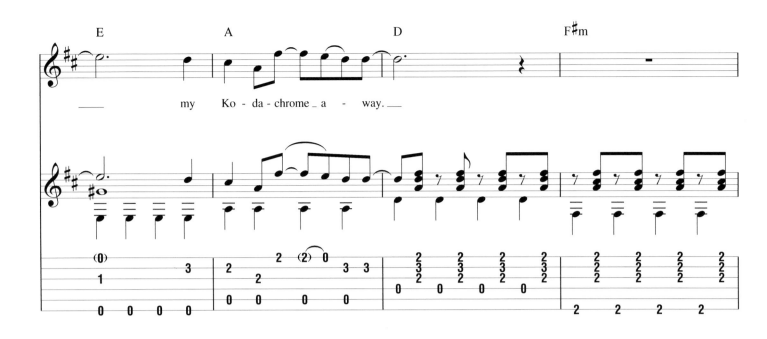

my Ko - da - chrome _ a - way. _

2. If you took all _ Ma - ma, don't _

Repeat and fade

Outro

take my Ko - da - chrome _ a - way. _____ Ma - ma, don't _

Landslide

Words and Music by Stevie Nicks

Mother Nature's Son

Words and Music by John Lennon and Paul McCartney

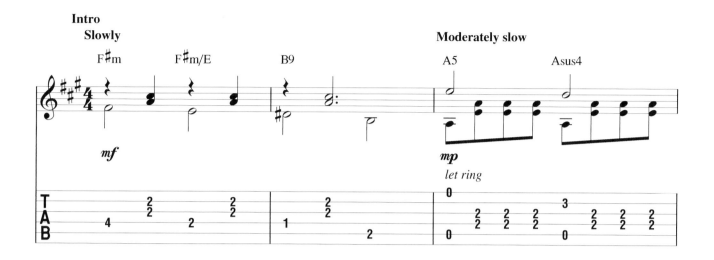

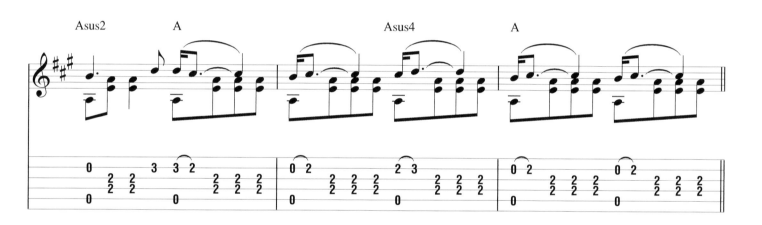

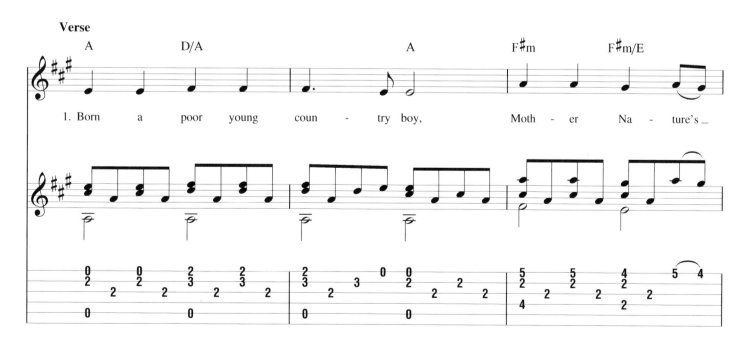

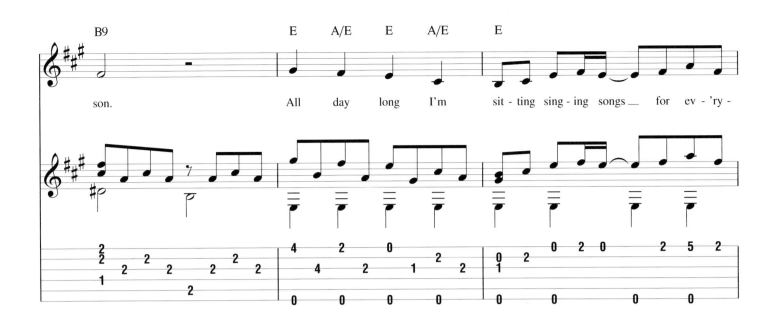

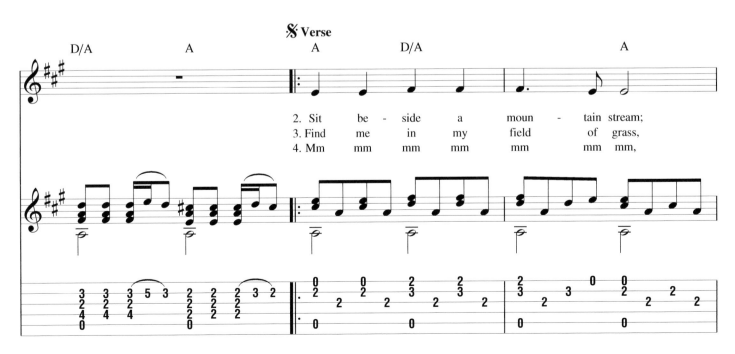

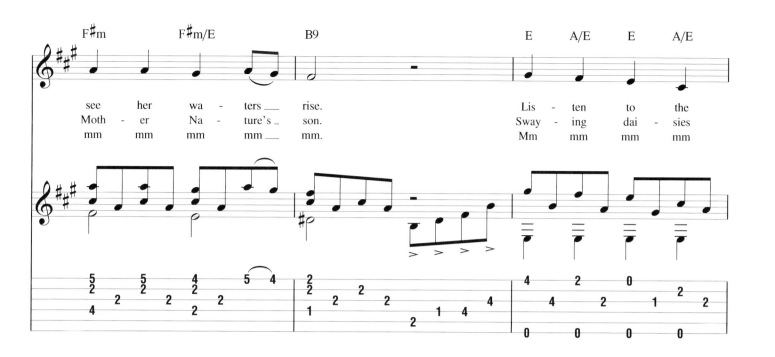

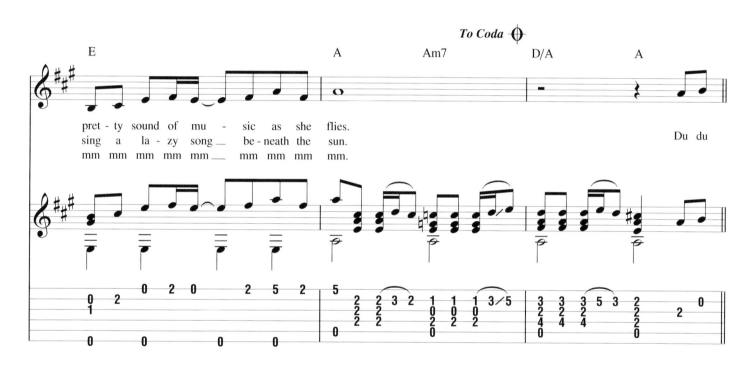

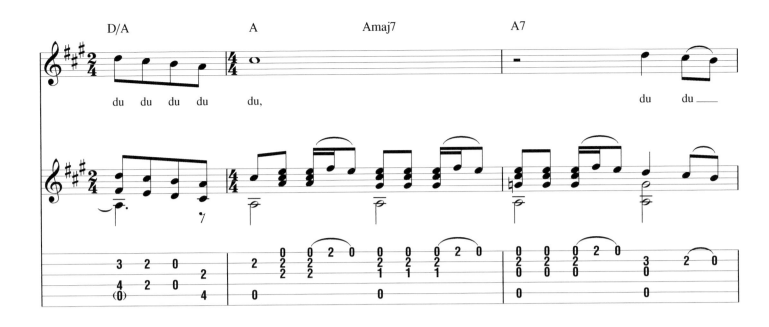

2nd time, D.S. al Coda

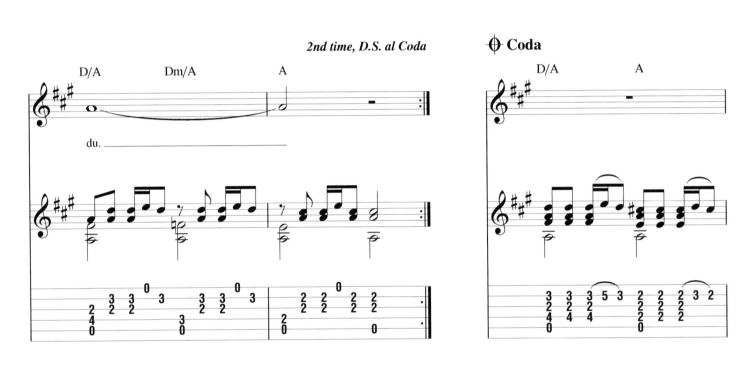

⊕ Coda

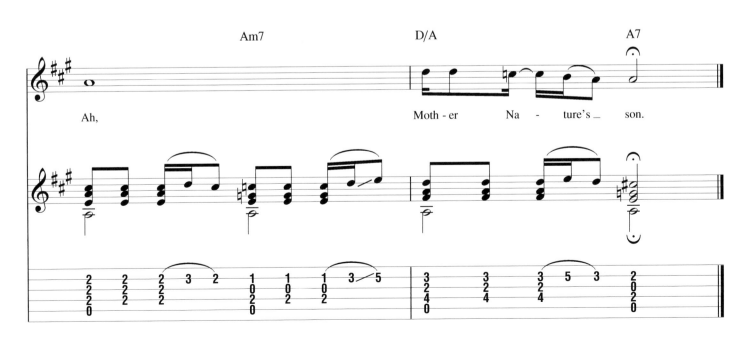

My Cherie Amour

Words and Music by Stevie Wonder, Sylvia Moy and Henry Cosby

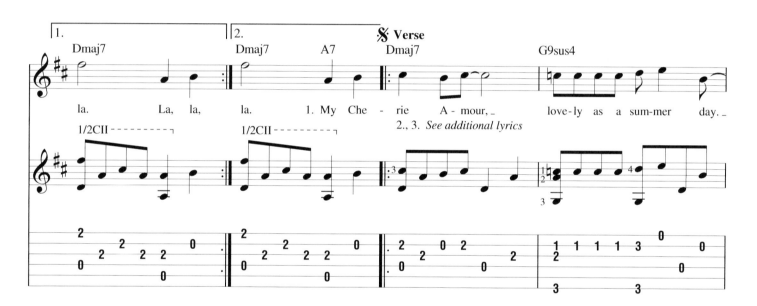

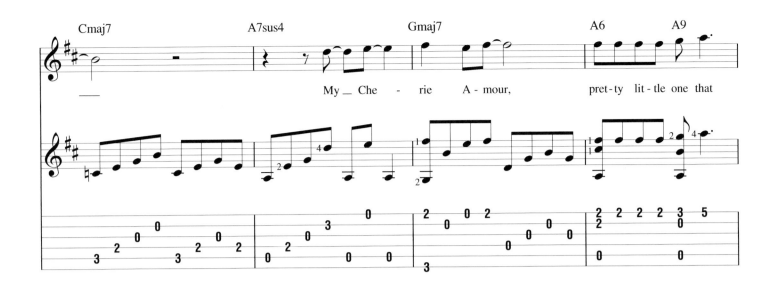

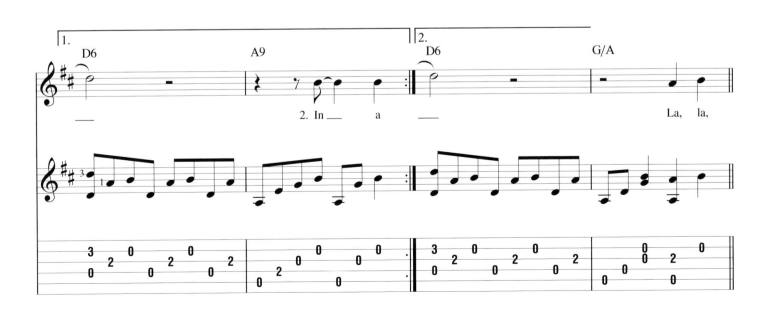

Interlude

D.S. al Coda

la, la, la, la. La, la, la, la, la. 3. May - be

Coda

Outro

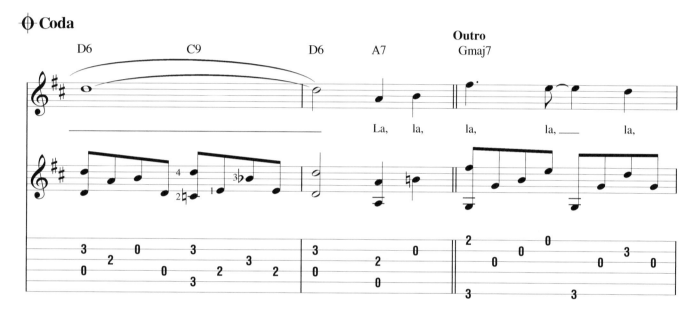

La, la, la, la, la,

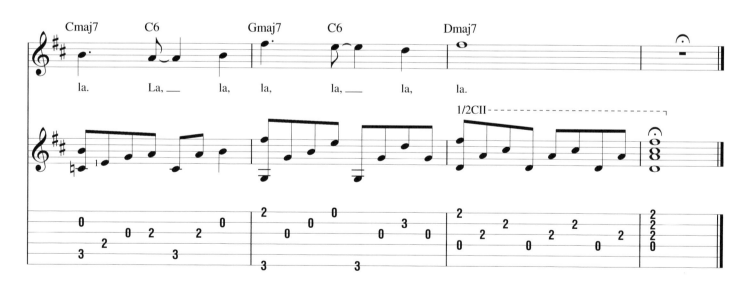

la. La, la, la, la, la, la.

Additional Lyrics

2. In a café or sometimes on a crowded street,
   I've been near you but you never noticed me.
   My Cherie Amour, won't you tell me how could you ignore,
   That behind that little smile I wore,
   How I wish that you were mine.

3. Maybe someday, you'll see my face among the crowd.
   Maybe someday, I'll share your little distant cloud.
   Oh, Cherie Amour, pretty little one that I adore,
   You're the only girl my heart beats for;
   How I wish that you were mine.

Mr. Tambourine Man

Words and Music by Bob Dylan

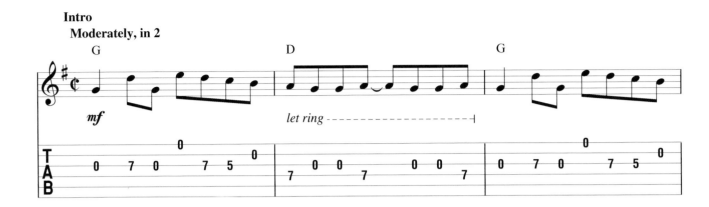

ain't   no   place ___   I'm   go - ing   to. ___

morn - ing   I'll ___ come

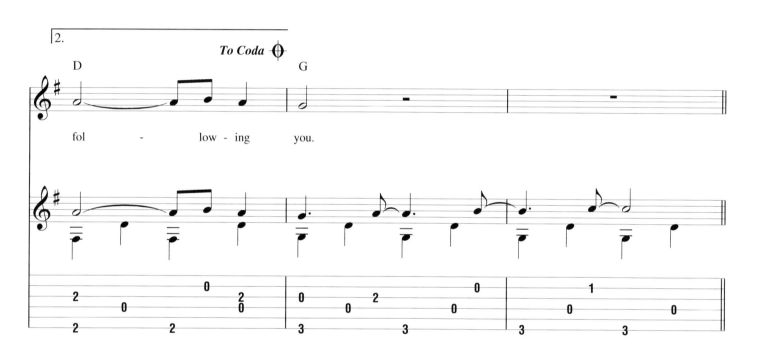

fol -   low - ing   you.

Verse

1. Take   me   for ___   a   trip   up - on ___ your   mag - ic   swirl - ing

read - y   to ___   go   an - y - where; ___ I'm   read - y   for ___ to

ship.   All my   sens - es   have __ been   stripped,   and my
fade   un -   to my   own __ pa -   rade.   Cast your

hands can't   feel ___ to   grip,   and my   toes too numb __ to
danc - ing   spell __ my

step.   Wait   on - ly   for ___ my   boot heels to ___ be

wan - der - ing. ___ 2. I'm way; I

D.S. al Coda
(take repeat)

prom - ise to ___ go un - der it. ___

Coda

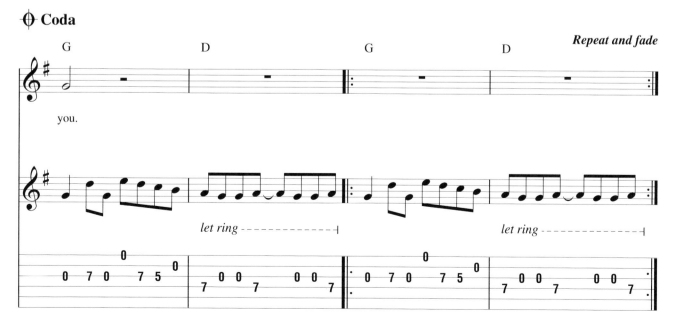

you.

let ring - - - - - - - - - -   *let ring - - - - - - - - - -*

Nights in White Satin

Words and Music by Justin Hayward

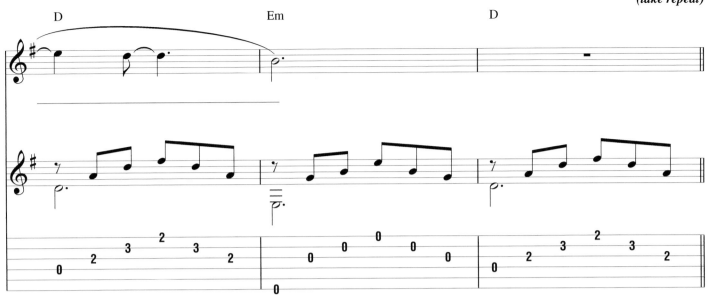

Ring of Fire

Words and Music by Merle Kilgore and June Carter

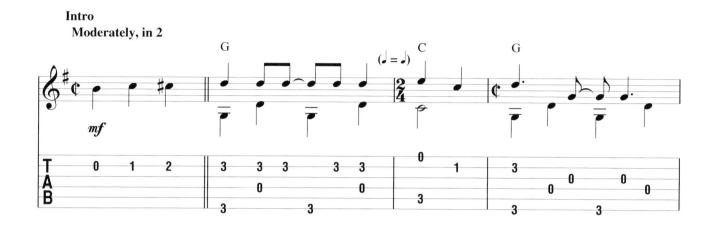

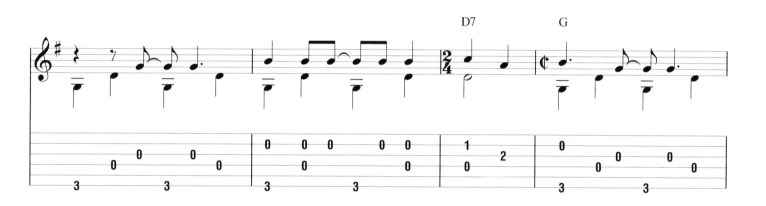

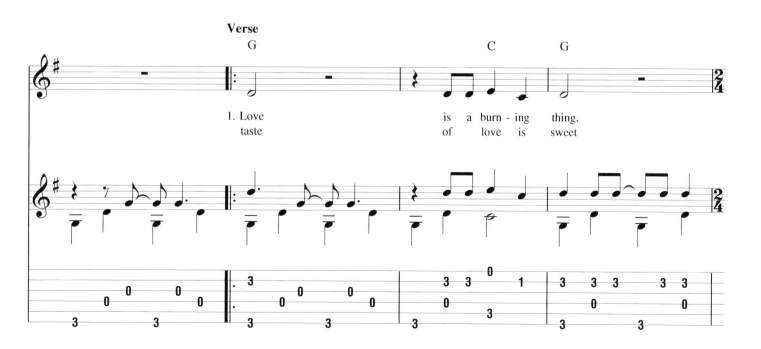

and it makes
when it makes hearts

a fier - y ring.
like ours___ beat.

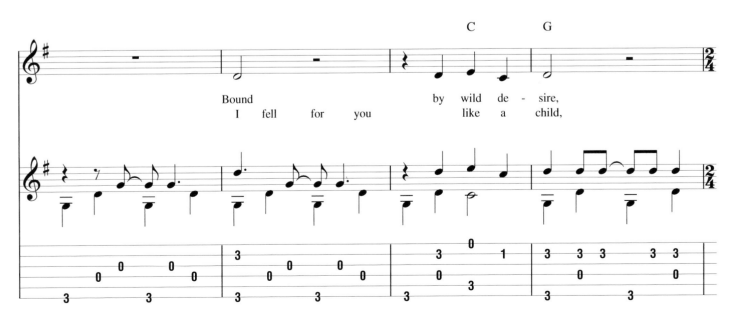

Bound by wild de - sire,
I fell for you like a child,

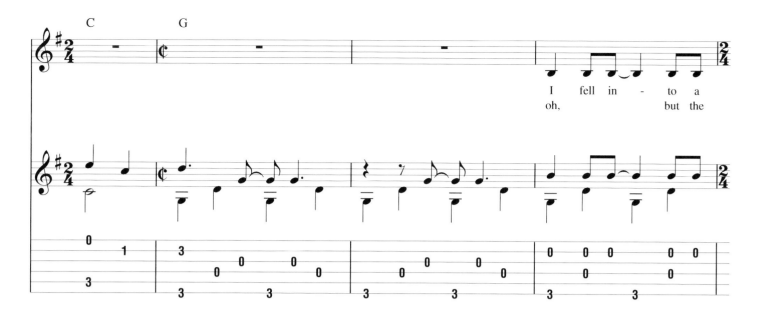

*Brush-up

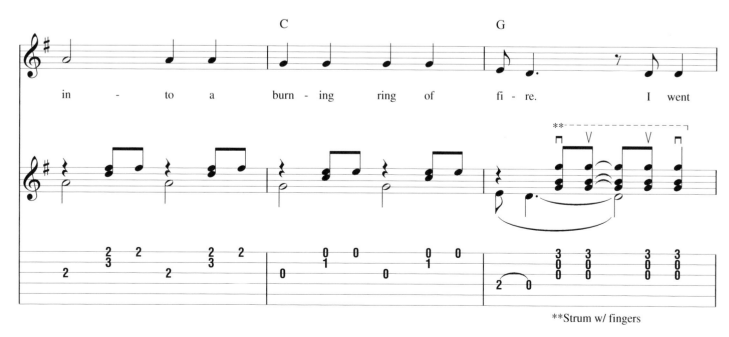

**Strum w/ fingers

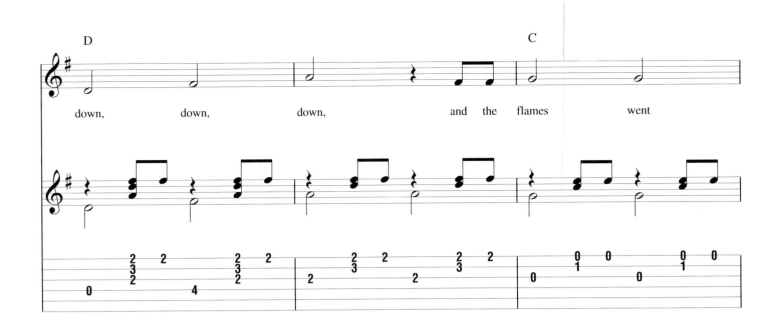

down, down, down, and the flames went

high - er. And it burns, burns, burns,

the ring of fi - re, the ring of

Repeat and fade

The Sound of Silence

Words and Music by Paul Simon

*Strum all upstem chords w/ fingers.

And the vi - sion _____ that was plant - ed in my
when my eyes were stabbed __ by the flash of a ne - on
But my words _____ like si - lent rain - drops

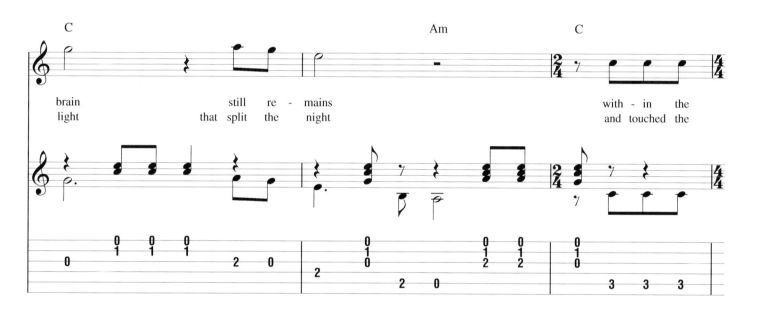

brain still re - mains with - in the
light that split the night and touched the

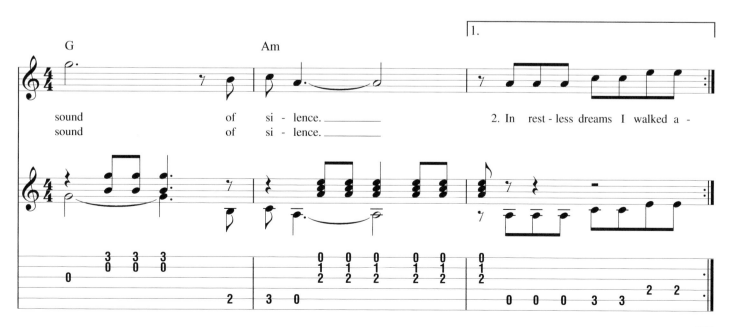

sound of si - lence. _____
sound of si - lence. _____ 2. In rest - less dreams I walked a -

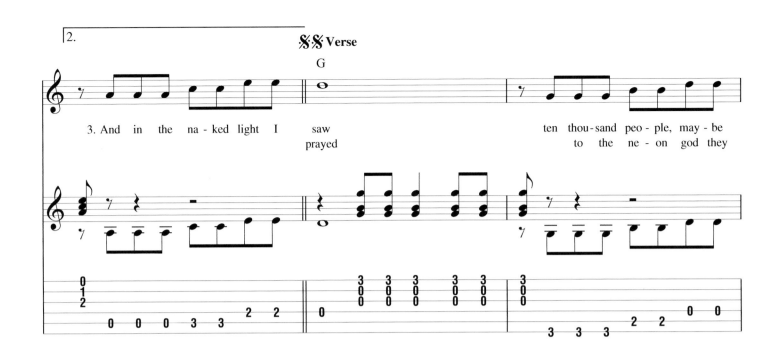

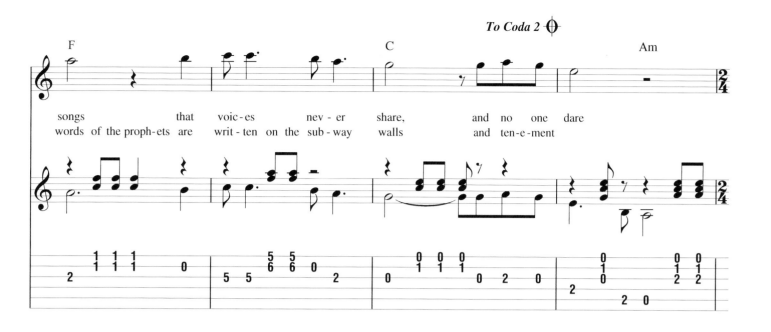

songs / words of the proph-ets are that voic-es writ-ten on the nev-er sub-way share, walls and no one and ten-e-ment dare

dis-turb the sound of si-lence. _____ 4. "Fools!" said I, "You do not

⊕ **Coda 1**

fell and ech-oed _____ in the

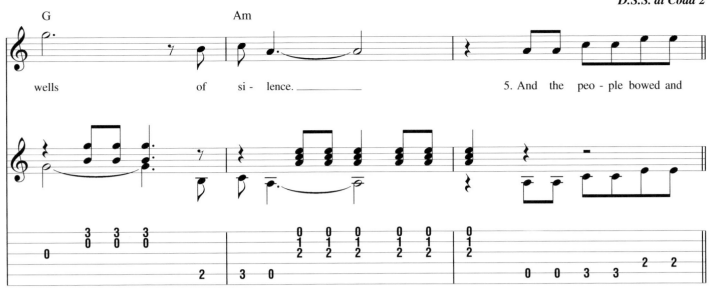

wells   of si - lence.   5. And the peo - ple bowed and

Coda 2

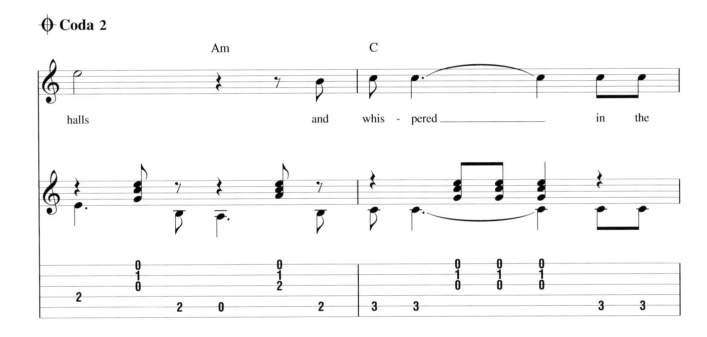

halls   and whis - pered   in the

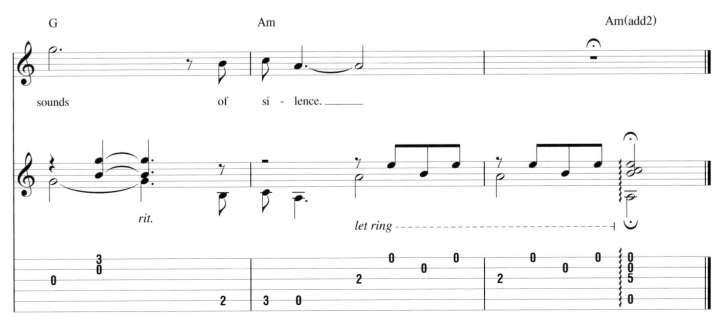

sounds   of si - lence.

rit.   *let ring*

Take Me Home, Country Roads

Words and Music by John Denver, Bill Danoff and Taffy Nivert

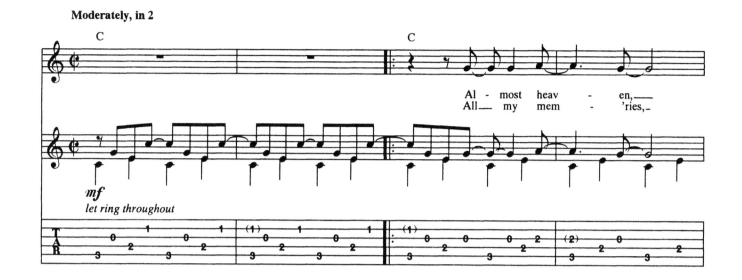

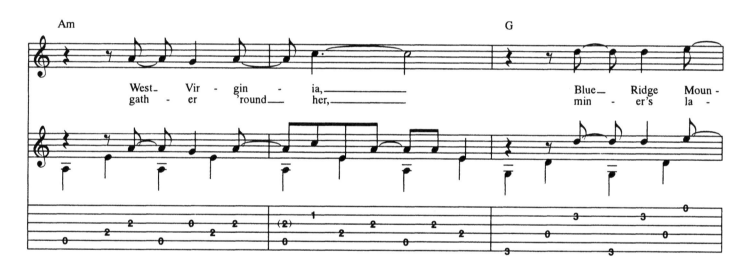

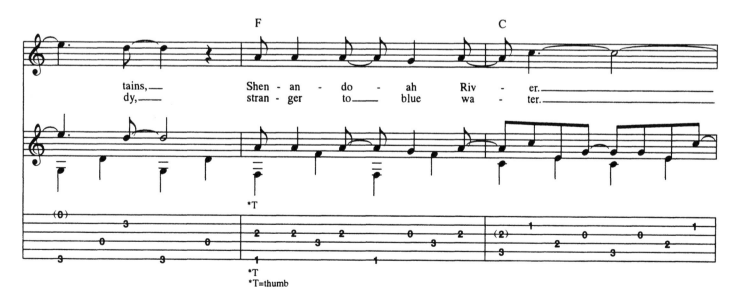

*T
*T=thumb

Time After Time

Words and Music by Cyndi Lauper and Rob Hyman

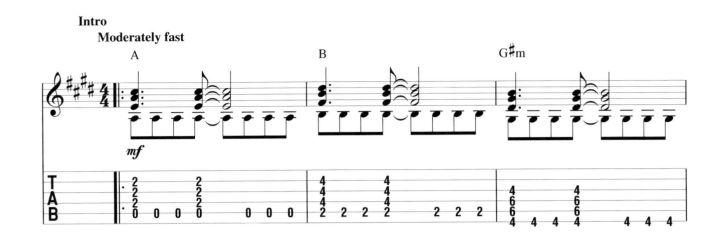

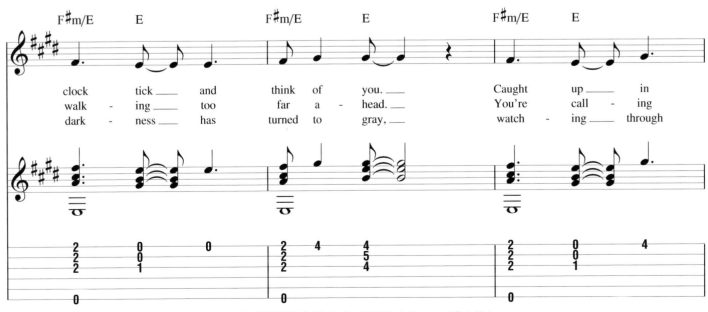

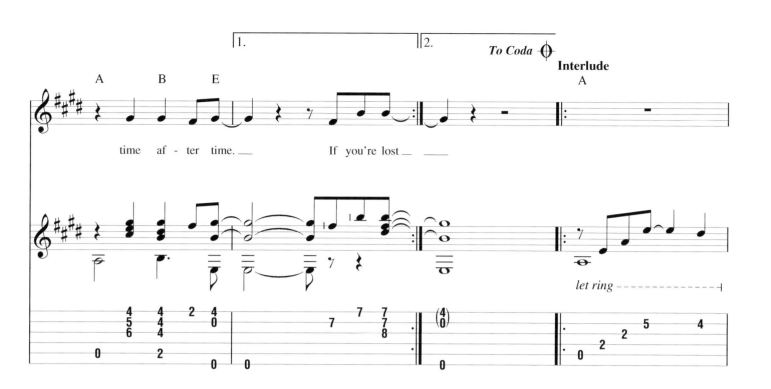

time af - ter time. ___ If you're lost ___

sim.

*Take 2nd ending on Verse;
take repeat on Chorus.

⊕ Coda

Repeat and fade

Time af - ter time. ___

Time in a Bottle

Words and Music by Jim Croce

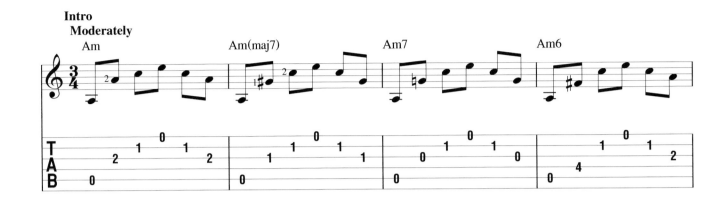

1. If

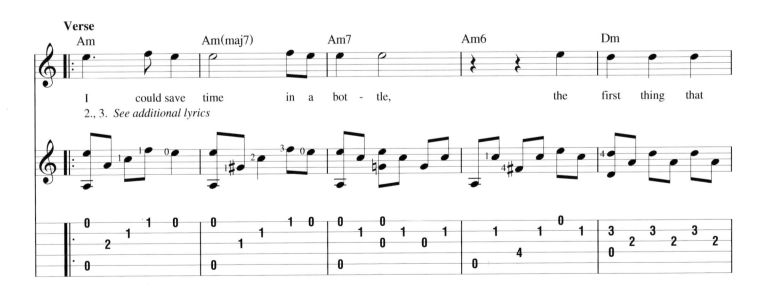

I could save time in a bottle, the first thing that

2., 3. *See additional lyrics*

Additional Lyrics

2. If I could make days last forever,
   If words could make wishes come true,
   I'd save ev'ry day like a treasure, and then
   Again I would spend them with you.

3. If I had a box just for wishes,
   And dreams that had never come ture,
   The box would be empty except for the mem'ry
   Of how they were answered by you.

Yesterday

Words and Music by John Lennon and Paul McCartney

Bridge

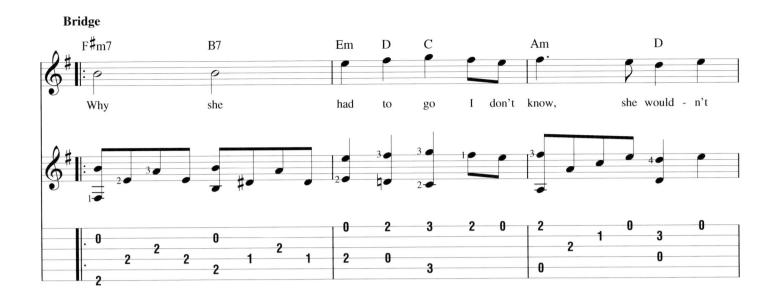

Why she had to go I don't know, she would-n't

say. I said some - thing wrong, now I

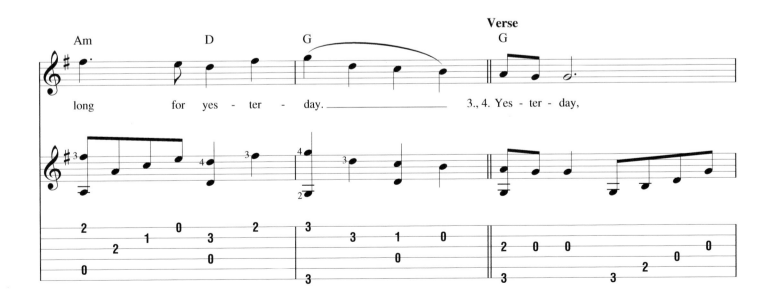

long for yes - ter - day. _____ 3., 4. Yes - ter - day,

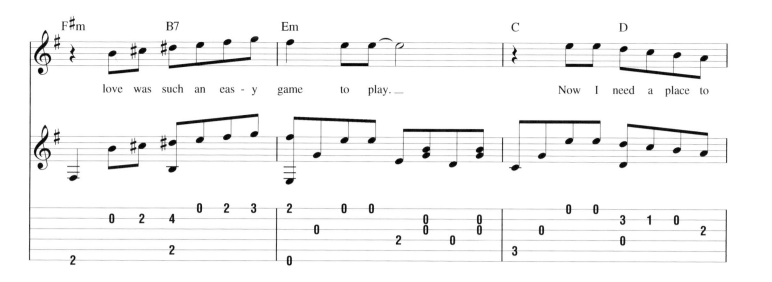

love was such an eas - y game to play. ___ Now I need a place to

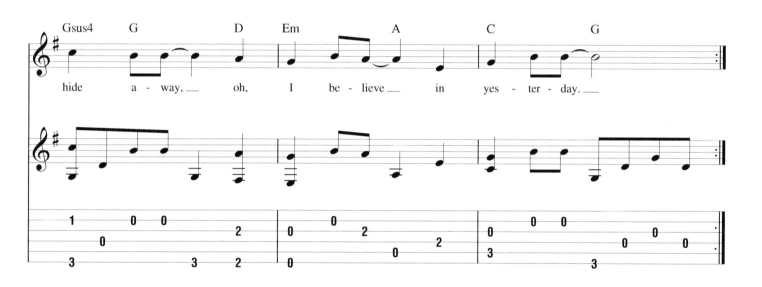

hide a - way, ___ oh, I be - lieve ___ in yes - ter - day. ___

Outro

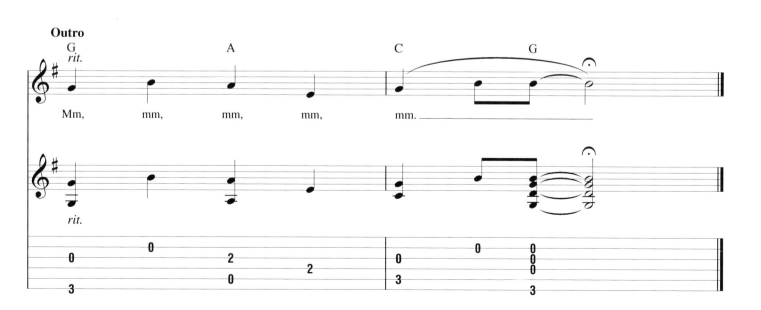

Mm, mm, mm, mm, mm. ___

You've Got a Friend

Words and Music by Carole King

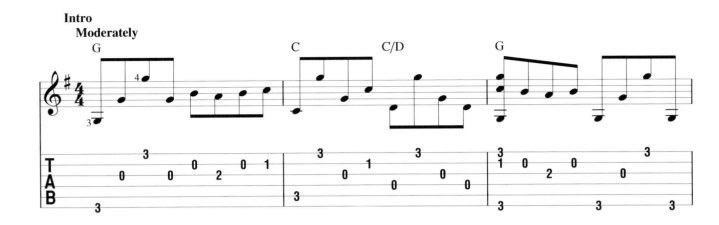

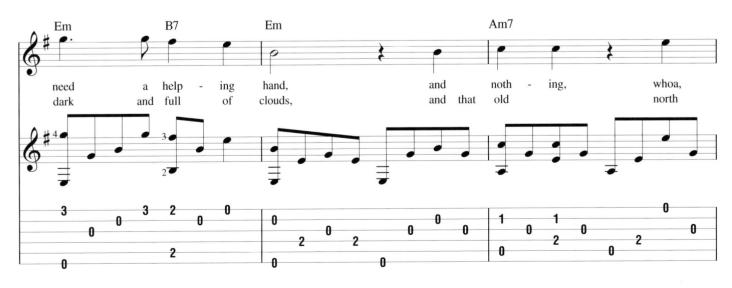

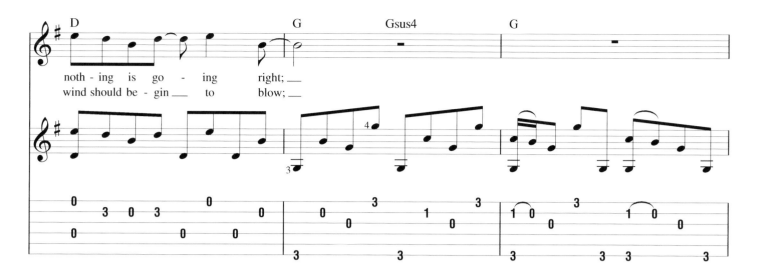

noth - ing is go - ing right; ___
wind should be - gin ___ to blow; ___

close your eyes ___ and think of me, and soon I will be
keep you head ___ to - geth - er and call my name out

there to bright-en up ___ e - ven your dark - est night. ___
loud, ___ now. Soon I'll be knock-in' up - on ___ your door. ___

FINGERPICKING GUITAR BOOKS

Hone your fingerpicking skills with these great songbooks featuring solo guitar arrangements in standard notation and tablature. The arrangements in these books are carefully written for intermediate-level guitarists. Each song combines melody and harmony in one superb guitar fingerpicking arrangement. Each book also includes an introduction to basic fingerstyle guitar.

FINGERPICKING ACOUSTIC
00699614...$14.99

FINGERPICKING ACOUSTIC CLASSICS
00160211...$14.99

FINGERPICKING ACOUSTIC HITS
00160202...$12.99

FINGERPICKING ACOUSTIC ROCK
00699764...$12.99

FINGERPICKING BALLADS
00699717...$12.99

FINGERPICKING BEATLES
00699049...$19.99

FINGERPICKING BEETHOVEN
00702390...$8.99

FINGERPICKING BLUES
00701277 ....$9.99

FINGERPICKING BROADWAY FAVORITES
00699843...$9.99

FINGERPICKING BROADWAY HITS
00699838...$7.99

FINGERPICKING CELTIC FOLK
00701148...$10.99

FINGERPICKING CHILDREN'S SONGS
00699712...$9.99

FINGERPICKING CHRISTIAN
00701076 ....$7.99

FINGERPICKING CHRISTMAS
00699599...$9.99

FINGERPICKING CHRISTMAS CLASSICS
00701695...$7.99

FINGERPICKING CHRISTMAS SONGS
00171333...$9.99

FINGERPICKING CLASSICAL
00699620...$10.99

FINGERPICKING COUNTRY
00699687...$10.99

FINGERPICKING DISNEY
00699711...$15.99

FINGERPICKING EARLY JAZZ STANDARDS
00276565 ....$12.99

FINGERPICKING DUKE ELLINGTON
00699845...$9.99

FINGERPICKING ENYA
00701161...$10.99

FINGERPICKING FILM SCORE MUSIC
00160143...$12.99

FINGERPICKING GOSPEL
00701059...$9.99

FINGERPICKING GUITAR BIBLE
00691040 ....$19.99

FINGERPICKING HIT SONGS
00160195...$12.99

FINGERPICKING HYMNS
00699688...$9.99

FINGERPICKING IRISH SONGS
00701965...$9.99

FINGERPICKING ITALIAN SONGS
00159778...$12.99

FINGERPICKING JAZZ FAVORITES
00699844...$9.99

FINGERPICKING JAZZ STANDARDS
00699840...$10.99

FINGERPICKING ELTON JOHN
00237495...$12.99

FINGERPICKING LATIN FAVORITES
00699842...$9.99

FINGERPICKING LATIN STANDARDS
00699837...$12.99

FINGERPICKING ANDREW LLOYD WEBBER
00699839...$14.99

FINGERPICKING LOVE SONGS
00699841...$12.99

FINGERPICKING LOVE STANDARDS
00699836 ....$9.99

FINGERPICKING LULLABYES
00701276...$9.99

FINGERPICKING MOVIE MUSIC
00699919...$10.99

FINGERPICKING MOZART
00699794...$9.99

FINGERPICKING POP
00699615...$12.99

FINGERPICKING POPULAR HITS
00139079...$12.99

FINGERPICKING PRAISE
00699714...$10.99

FINGERPICKING ROCK
00699716...$12.99

FINGERPICKING STANDARDS
00699613...$12.99

FINGERPICKING WEDDING
00699637...$9.99

FINGERPICKING WORSHIP
00700554...$10.99

FINGERPICKING NEIL YOUNG – GREATEST HITS
00700134...$14.99

FINGERPICKING YULETIDE
00699654...$9.99

HAL•LEONARD®

Visit Hal Leonard online at **www.halleonard.com**

Prices, contents and availability
subject to change without notice.